Aus der Geschichte lernen
How to Learn from History

Verleihung des Blätter-Demokratiepreises 1997

Herausgegeben von Karl D. Bredthauer und Arthur Heinrich

edition Blätter 2

edition Blätter.

CIP-Kurztitelaufnahme der Deutschen Bibliothek:

Aus der Geschichte lernen – How to Learn from History
Verleihung des „Blätter"-Demokratiepreises 1997 an Daniel Jonah Goldhagen: eine Dokumentation / Karl D. Bredthauer und Arthur Heinrich (Hg.). Mit Reden von Jürgen Habermas, Jan Philipp Reemtsma und Daniel Jonah Goldhagen.
- Bonn: Blätter Verl.-Ges., 1997 (edition Blätter; 2)

edition Blätter 2
2., unveränderte Auflage, Bonn 2000
Druck: Leppelt Druck + Repro GmbH, Bonn

Postfach 2831, 53018 Bonn
Tel. 0228 650133, Fax 0228 650251

ISBN 3-9804925-1-6

Bonn, Beethovenhalle, 10. März. Daniel Jonah Goldhagen erhält den Demokratiepreis 1997.
Foto: AP/Fritz Reiss

Inhalt

Vorbemerkung

Am 10. März 1997 ging der Demokratiepreis der „Blätter für deutsche und internationale Politik“ und ihres Fördervereins an Daniel Jonah Goldhagen, Autor des Buches *Hitler's Willing Executioners (Hitlers willige Vollstrecker).*

Nach einem Empfang der Bonner Oberbürgermeisterin für Preisträger, Laudatoren und zahlreiche Gäste fand anschließend die Preisverleihung in einer mit über 2 000 Zuhörern restlos ausverkauften Beethovenhalle statt, eine Veranstaltung, die im In- und Ausland große Beachtung fand.

Mit dem Band *Aus der Geschichte lernen/How to Learn from History* legen wir erstmals eine Gesamtdokumentation des Ereignisses vor: die Reden der Laudatoren Jürgen Habermas und Jan Philipp Reemtsma sowie die Dankesworte des Preisträgers in deutscher und englischer Sprache, darüber hinaus eine ausführliche Wiedergabe des Presseechos in der Bundesrepublik.

Preliminary Note

On March 10, 1997, the “Blätter für deutsche und internationale Politik” [“Journal for German and International Politics”] and its supporters' association awarded their Democracy Prize to Daniel Jonah Goldhagen, author of *Hitler's Willing Executioners: Ordinary Germans and the Holocaust.*

Following a reception by Bonn's Lord Mayor for the honoree, his laudators and numerous prominent guests, the award ceremony itself occured in the city's Beethovenhalle in front of a standing room only audience of over 2,000 people. The event attracted much attention in Germany as well as abroad.

With this volume *Aus der Geschichte lernen/How to Learn from History* the “Blätter” publish for the very first time a complete documentation of this event consisting of the speeches delivered by Mr. Goldhagen's laudators, Jürgen Habermas, and Jan Philipp Reemtsma, as well as the honoree's reply and acceptance speech published in German as well as English. The documentation also comprises a detailed selection of the media reaction in the Federal Republic to this event.

Die Herausgeber/The Editors

Volles Haus, vorne v. l. n. r.: Ute Habermas, Jürgen Habermas, Joschka Fischer. Foto: Josef Menzen

Karl D. Bredthauer

Limits of a German Normalization

The Constitutive Meaning of the Break of 1945/49

At the opening of the ceremony on the evening of March 10, 1997, Karl D. Bredthauer, on behalf of the editors and the board of trustees of the "Blätter", offered the following reflections on the political context in which Daniel Jonah Goldhagen was awarded the Democracy Prize.

Allow me, ladies and gentlemen, a few brief remarks on the Democracy Prize for 1997, and on the intentions of the editors and the board of trustees of the "Blätter." As you know, the prize last went to the citizens' movement in the former GDR. That was in 1990, in Berlin. We gather today in Bonn – the city whose name the constitution bears – before the background of the transformation that began at that time, from the Bonn Republic into the Berlin Republic. (Some may criticize our use of the controversial formula "Berlin Republic"; perhaps it would really be better to speak of a transition of the Federal Republic into a new *stage*, into the Berlin stage of its development.)

There has been a great deal speculation, much of it premature, concerning what has since been named the "turn" of 1989/90. (Here we will only make passing note of the thoughtless disregard of the democratic movement, and its motto "*We* are the people", and the erasure of all citizens' initiatives, audible in today's omnipresent talk of the anonymous "turn"!)

There has thus been a great many who expect that the democratic break of 1989 would "historicize" the caesura of May 8, 1945; that it

Karl D. Bredthauer

Grenzen einer deutschen Normalisierung

Die konstitutive Bedeutung des Bruchs von 1945/49

Zu Beginn der „ceremony“ am Abend des 10. März 1997 trug Karl D. Bredthauer im Namen der Redaktion und des Fördervereins der „Blätter“ folgende Gedanken zum politischen Kontext der Demokratiepreis-Verleihung an Daniel Jonah Goldhagen vor.

Gestatten Sie mir, meine Damen und Herren, einige kurze Bemerkungen zum Demokratiepreis 1997, zu den Intentionen von Redaktion und Förderverein der „Blätter“. Zuletzt ging der Preis, wie Sie wissen, an die Bürgerbewegung der damaligen DDR. Das war 1990 in Berlin. Wenn wir uns heute hier in Bonn versammeln – der Stadt, deren Namen das Grundgesetz trägt – und Daniel Jonah Goldhagen ehren, so tun wir dies vor dem Hintergrund der seither in Gang gekommenen Verwandlung der Bonner in eine Berliner Republik. (Manche kritisieren übrigens, daß wir die umstrittene Formel von der Berliner Republik aufgegriffen haben; vielleicht sollten wir wirklich besser vom Übergang der Bundesrepublik in ein neues *Stadium*, in das Berliner Stadium ihrer Entwicklung sprechen.)

Nicht wenige, oft unausgegorene Spekulationen knüpfen sich an die mittlerweile so genannte „Wende“ von 1989/90. (Notieren wir hier nur am Rande, welch unbedachte Mißachtung der Demokratiebewegung und ihrer Devise „*Wir* sind das Volk“ in diesem heute allgegenwärtigen, alle Bürgerinitiative wegwischenden Unwort von der anonymen „Wende“ mitschwingt!)

Nicht wenige also erwarten, der demokratische Umbruch von 1989 werde die Zäsur des 8. Mai 1945 „historisieren“, die deutsche Katastrophe rela-

would relativize the German catastrophe and bridge the gulf that separates our republic from that other, justly destroyed Germany. (This leads to questionable comparisons between two German pasts. – Or are we supposed to speak of *three* German pasts? In view of a Bonn Republic that is itself already undergoing "historicization"?)

Some dream of a German normalcy beyond the "old" Federal Republic, which in their view shrinks into a sort of occupying regime, and, in a peculiar equation with the GDR, has already been overcome, or should be overcome as quickly as possible – as a last, unworthy intermezzo of Germany's loss of sovereignty.

Daniel Goldhagen's book and the debate it touched off have, at the right moment, reminded us of the entire magnitude of that singular political-moral catastrophe; a catastrophe that was ended in 1945 with the necessary, more than deserved, and globally welcomed destruction of a Germany that ought never to have existed.

But have we all really understood? Have we understood what historical act of mercy – I won't shrink from using that pathetic word at this point –, what courage – of the victorious forces, the victims and their relatives, the neighboring peoples – we Germans have to thank for the republic in which we live? With all deliberate bluntness: this German Federal Republic is a gift that must still be deserved. A gift not least from the country from which this day's awardee has come. (Some find in this reference to the special relationship between the Federal Republic of Germany and the United States a diminution of the role of other participants in the anti-Hitler coalition, particularly the Soviet Union. That is beside the point. For me it is much more a matter of realizing that it behooves no one, neither on the left nor on other sides of the political spectrum, to disparage this German-American special relationship, which is simply fundamental for the Federal Republic.)

Daniel Jonah Goldhagen's achievement consists in his reminding us of the responsibility of the individual – for all that he does, even for what he doesn't do, doesn't collaborate in – and in his refusal to accept the usual

tivieren und die Kluft einebnen, die unsere Republik von jenem zu Recht untergegangenen Deutschland abgrenzt. (Dabei kommt es zu fragwürdigen Vergleichen zwischen zwei deutschen Vergangenheiten – oder müssen wir, mit Blick auf eine ebenfalls schon der „Historisierung" unterzogene Bonner Republik, von *drei* deutschen Vergangenheiten sprechen?)

Manche träumen von einer deutschen Normalität jenseits der „alten" Bundesrepublik, die in ihrer Optik zu einer Art Besatzungsregime schrumpft und, in seltsamer „Gleichstellung" mit der DDR, überwunden ist oder doch so schnell wie möglich überwunden werden sollte – als ein letztlich unwürdiges Intermezzo deutscher „Fremdbestimmung".

Daniel Goldhagens Buch und die von ihm angestoßene Debatte haben uns – zur rechten Zeit – das ganze Ausmaß jener singulären politisch-moralischen Katastrophe ins Gedächtnis gerufen, die 1945 mit der notwendigen, mehr als verdienten, von der ganzen Welt mit Aufatmen begrüßten Zerschlagung eines Deutschland enden mußte, das nie wieder erstehen darf.

Aber haben wirklich alle begriffen? Haben wir verstanden, welchem – ich scheue das pathetische Wort an diesem Punkt nicht – Gnadenakt der Geschichte, welcher Großmut – der Siegermächte, der Opfer und ihrer Angehörigen, der Nachbarvölker – wir Deutschen die Republik verdanken, in der wir leben? Diese Bundesrepublik Deutschland ist – in aller vermeintlichen Glanzlosigkeit – ein Geschenk, das noch verdient sein will. Ein Geschenk nicht zuletzt jenes Landes, aus dem der Preisträger des heutigen Tages zu uns gekommen ist. (Manche sehen in dem Hinweis auf das Sonderverhältnis zwischen der Bundesrepublik Deutschland und den Vereinigten Staaten eine Minderung der Rolle anderer Teilnehmer der Anti-Hitler-Koalition, besonders der Sowjetunion. Darum geht es nicht. Es geht mir vielmehr um die Einsicht, daß eine Herabwürdigung jenes – für die Bundesrepublik nun einmal fundamentalen – deutsch-amerikanischen Sonderverhältnisses auf die überwundene Konstellation des Kalten Krieges niemandem gut zu Gesicht steht, weder der Linken, noch anderen Seiten des politischen Spektrums.)

Daniel Jonah Goldhagens Verdienst liegt auch darin, daß er die Verantwortung des Einzelnen – für alles, was er tut oder eben nicht tut, nicht mitmacht – in Erinnerung ruft und das übliche Sichverstecken hinter Be-

self-concealment behind orders and obedience. Whoever argues that this standard of civil rights and civic duty is not appropriate to the situation of Wehrmacht soldiers, or of the neighbors of those whom the Gestapo rounded up, carried off and murdered, *emphasizes* precisely what Kurt Sontheimer evoked with such urgency as the *constitutive* meaning of the break between that Germany and our Federal Republic, a break that no "normalization" can lead behind. There is no German "reinstatement into the previous condition." Our good fortune and our opportunity for the future lie in something entirely different – and it is astonishing how defensively some have reacted to Goldhagen, as he reminds us of just this: all normalcy of the Federal Republic lies in its firm integration into the West, in its "internationalization," to use a concept that the awardee himself will explain here this evening. Bonn is not Weimar, and did not become Weimar, and Berlin is neither justified nor damned in replaying the role of capital city. A Berlin that accepts its new definition – as the federal capital of a Western republic and never again as the point of origin of a German special path – would represent a historical chance: that *all* Germans will finally, really *arrive* in the political civilization of modernity. Modernity's contradictions can be our collective lot and our collective work, with friends like Daniel Goldhagen...

Translation by Max Pensky

fehl und Gehorsam nicht hinnimmt. Wer meint, dieser Maßstab von Bürgerrechten und Bürgerpflichten werde der Situation nicht gerecht, in der sich etwa die Soldaten der Wehrmacht befanden oder die Nachbarn derer, die von der Gestapo abgeholt, verschleppt, ermordet wurden – der *unterstreicht* doch gerade die – von Kurt Sontheimer so eindringlich beschworene – *konstitutive* Bedeutung des Bruchs zwischen jenem Deutschland und unserer Bundesrepublik, hinter den keine „Normalisierung“ zurückführt. Es gibt keine deutsche „Wiedereinsetzung in den vorigen Stand“. Unser Glück, unsere Zukunftschancen liegen in etwas ganz anderem – und es verblüfft, wie abwehrend manche auf Goldhagen reagieren, wenn eben dieser uns daran erinnert: Alle Normalität der Bundesrepublik liegt in ihrer festen Einbindung in den Westen, in ihrer „Internationalisierung“ – um einen Begriff zu verwenden, den der Preisträger heute abend hier explizieren wird. Bonn ist nicht Weimar, ist nicht Weimar geworden, und Berlin ist weder berechtigt noch etwa verdammt, die Hauptstadtrolle als Replay zu geben. Ein Berlin, das seine neue Bestimmung annimmt – Bundeshauptstadt einer westlichen Republik zu werden und nie wieder Startplatz deutscher Sonderwege –, stünde für eine historische Chance: daß *alle* Deutschen endlich wirklich *ankommen* in der politischen Zivilisation der Moderne. An deren Widersprüchen arbeiten wir uns dann gemeinsam ab, mit Freunden wie Daniel Goldhagen …

Jürgen Habermas

On the Public Use of History

Why a "Democracy Prize" for Daniel Goldhagen?

The Democracy Prize, last awarded in 1990 to Bärbel Bohley and Wolfgang Ullmann on behalf of the civil rights activists of the DDR, is given to this year's recipient on the following grounds: through the "urgency, the forcefulness, and the moral strength of his presentation" Daniel Goldhagen has "provided a powerful stimulus to the public conscience of the Federal Republic"; he has sharpened "our sensibility for what constitutes the background and the limit of a German 'normalization.'" This reference to the rhetorical effect of the book, and to the controversial issue of normalization (which poses itself anew in the transition to a Berlin Republic) makes clear what the Board of Trustees of the *Blätter für deutsche und internationale Politik* has in mind in awarding this prize – and what it does not. It cannot and will not enter into a controversy amongst professional historians. In Germany as well as the United States, a number of prominent historians have contributed greatly to the research of the Nazi period, and to the political enlightenment of German citizens concerning the complex pre-history of the Holocaust, often with the devotion of an entire professional career. Here I will name only Martin Broszat, Hans Mommsen and Eberhart Jäckel, and younger historians such as Ulrich Herbert, Dietrich Pohl and Thomas Sandkühler as representative. The question is not who among contemporary historians *deserves* the attention of a wider public, but rather how we are to understand the unusual degree of public attention that Daniel Goldhagen's book has in

Jürgen Habermas

Über den öffentlichen Gebrauch der Historie

Warum ein „Demokratiepreis" für Daniel Goldhagen?

Der Demokratiepreis, den zuletzt 1990 Bärbel Bohley und Wolfgang Ullmann für die Bürgerrechtler der DDR entgegengenommen haben, geht an den diesjährigen Preisträger mit der folgenden Begründung: Daniel Goldhagen habe „aufgrund der Eindringlichkeit und der moralischen Kraft seiner Darstellung dem öffentlichen Bewußtsein in der Bundesrepublik wesentliche Impulse gegeben"; er habe „die Sensibilität für Hintergründe und Grenzen einer deutschen ‚Normalisierung'" geschärft. Die Bezugnahme auf die rhetorische Wirkung des Buches und auf die Streitfrage der Normalisierung, die sich im Übergang zur Berliner Republik erneut stellt, läßt erkennen, was das Kuratorium der „Blätter für deutsche und internationale Politik" mit dieser Preisverleihung im Sinn hat – und was nicht. Es kann und will nicht in eine wissenschaftliche Kontroverse eingreifen. Auch in Deutschland haben sich bedeutende Historiker, oft mit der Energie eines ganzen akademischen Lebens, um die Erforschung der Nazi-Zeit und um die politische Aufklärung der Bürger über die komplexe Vorgeschichte des Holocaust große Verdienste erworben. Stellvertretend nenne ich nur Martin Broszat, Hans Mommsen und Eberhard Jaeckel sowie unter den Jüngeren Ulrich Herbert, Dietrich Pohl und Thomas Sandkühler. Die Frage ist nicht, wer von den Zeithistorikern die Aufmerksamkeit einer breiten Leserschaft verdient hätte, sondern wie die ungewöhnliche Aufmerksamkeit interessierter Bürger zu bewerten ist, die das Buch von Daniel Goldhagen tatsächlich gefunden hat.

fact received. Awarding this prize communicates the conviction that the public response that both book and author have found in the Federal Republic is as deserved as it is welcome.

This view has been the subject of vehement dispute. The book, so it is claimed by its detractors, offers a global and one-dimensional presentation of a highly complex event, thus satisfying the mass public's demand for oversimplified explanations. It is objected that the book employs an aesthetics of the gruesome as a stylistic tool, generating emotional effects that dim the capacity for sober judgment. Other criticisms refer less to the text itself and far more to the motives of those who buy and read it. Here we encounter the familiar stereotypes: "do-goodism," "negative nationalism", "flight from history." With a retrospective identification with the victims, so it is said, the descendants of the perpetrators have gotten themselves a cost-free and self-justifying kind of satisfaction, or again seize the opportunity to reject their own tradition, and to flee into the chimerical dream of a post-national nation. I must confess that I do not entirely understand these agitated reactions. They are trying to explain a phenomenon that stands in no need of explanation.

Clearly, a broad public response to a book such as this cannot come as a great surprise: one need only see how Goldhagen's analytical case histories of the annihilation of the Jews mesh with the expectations of a reading public as it searches for an understanding of this criminal chapter of its history. Goldhagen's investigations are tailored to address precisely those questions that have polarized our public and private discussions for the past half-century. From the very beginnings of the Federal Republic, there has been a fundamental disagreement between all those who would rather interpret the breakdown of civilization as if it were a natural event, on the one side, and those on the other side who insist on seeing it as the consequence of the actions of responsible persons – and not just of Hitler and his inner circle. Today, both sides square off with mutual suspicions of each others' respective motives: the diagnosis of denial thus stands opposed to the accusation of self-righteous moralizing. This hopeless battle only serves to conceal the truly fundamental question at issue: what does it mean to assign the responsibility for historical crimes retrospectively – if it is just this reckoning that we are now undertaking with the goal of

Der performative Sinn der Preisverleihung besagt, daß die öffentliche Resonanz, die Buch und Autor in der Bundesrepublik gefunden haben, ebenso verdient wie begrüßenswert ist.

Diese Aussage stößt auf vehementen Widerspruch. Das Buch, so heißt es, befriedige mit einer globalen und einebnenden Darstellung eines komplexen Geschehens das Bedürfnis des Massenpublikums nach vereinfachenden Erklärungen. Mit Stilmitteln einer Ästhetik der Grausamkeit erziele es emotionale Wirkungen, mit obszönen Schilderungen verdunkele es das Urteilsvermögen. Andere Vorwürfe beziehen sich weniger auf den Text als vielmehr auf die Motive der Käufer und Leser. Hier begegnen wir den bekannten Stereotypen von „Gutmenschentum", „negativem Nationalismus" und „Auszug aus der Geschichte". Die Nachkommen der Täter verschafften sich durch die nachträgliche Identifikation mit den Opfern eine kostenlos-selbstgerechte Genugtuung. Sie ergriffen wieder einmal die Gelegenheit, die Loyalität zu eigenen Überlieferungen aufzukündigen und ins schimärisch Postnationale zu flüchten. Ich muß gestehen, daß ich diese aufgeregten Reaktionen nicht verstehe. Sie versuchen, ein Phänomen zu erklären, das keiner Erklärung bedarf.

Eine breite Resonanz auf ein solches Buch war trivialerweise zu erwarten. Man muß sich nur klarmachen, wie beides ineinandergreift: Goldhagens analytische Fallstudien zur Judenvernichtung und die Erwartungshaltung eines Publikums, das an der Aufklärung dieses kriminellen Kapitels seiner Geschichte interessiert ist. Goldhagens Untersuchungen sind genau auf die Fragen zugeschnitten, die unsere privaten wie öffentlichen Diskussionen seit einem halben Jahrhundert polarisieren. Seit den Anfängen der Bundesrepublik besteht ein Gegensatz zwischen denen, die den Zivilisationsbruch lieber wie ein Naturereignis aus den Umständen erklären, und denen, die ihn eher verantwortlich handelnden Personen zuschreiben, und zwar nicht nur Hitler und seiner engsten Clique. Heute begegnen sich beide Parteien mit wechselseitigen Motivunterstellungen: der Diagnose der Verleugnung steht der Vorwurf selbstgerechter Moralisierung gegenüber. Dieser heillose Streit verdeckt die zugrundeliegende Frage: Was bedeutet überhaupt eine retrospektive Zurechnung von Verbrechen, die wir heute zum Zwecke einer ethisch-politischen Selbstverständigung unter Bürgern vornehmen? Gold-

generating an ethical-political process of public self-understanding? Goldhagen provides a new stimulus to a reflection about the proper public use of history.

In public discourses of self-understanding, which can be touched off by films, television series or exhibitions just as much as by historical works or "affairs," we argue not so much over short-terms goals and policies as over the forms of a desired political existence, and over the values that shall predominate in it. Moreover, such discourses concern how we as citizens of the Federal Republic can have mutual respect for one another, and how we wish to be acknowledged by others. National history constitutes an important background for this. National traditions and mentalities reach back far behind the origins of this Republic, forming a part of our personal identities. This connection between political self-understanding and historical awareness also determines the point of view from which Goldhagen's book is relevant for us. This singular crime – a crime that first generated the notion of a "crime against humanity" – has issued from the very midst of our collective life. For this reason, all those members of later generations who struggle to come to terms with their political existence in this country confront the same question: can the responsibility for mass political criminality ever be laid as a burden on individual persons or groups of persons? If so, who were the responsible actors, and what were their reasons for acting as they did? And insofar as normative justifications were of decisive importance for the actors, were these rooted in the culture, and in particular ways of thinking?

Goldhagen ascribes to a representative group of somehow convinced perpetrators a subjective justification for their acts that formed an integral part of the basic cultural convictions that were dominant at the time: "The rupture in the German cultural fabric that the Jews represented to Germans … was such that cultural taboos failed to hold sway when the Germans discussed the Jews."[1] This cannot but have a powerful impact on our own

1 Daniel Goldhagen, Hitler's Willing Executioners: Ordinary Germans and the Holocaust, New York 1996/Hitlers willige Vollstrecker, Berlin 1996, 63/87. [trans: bracketed references in the text subsequently refer to the American and German editions; when only one reference is given, it is to the German edition only and appears in my translation.]

hagen gibt einen weiteren Impuls zum Nachdenken über den richtigen öffentlichen Gebrauch der Historie.

In Diskursen der Selbstverständigung, die durch Filme, Fernsehserien und Ausstellungen ebenso wie durch historische Darstellungen oder „Affairen" angeregt werden, streiten wir uns nicht über kurzfristige Ziele und Politiken, sondern über Formen des erwünschten politischen Zusammenlebens, auch über die Werte, die im politischen Gemeinwesen Vorrang haben sollen. Gleichzeitig geht es darum, in welchen Hinsichten wir uns als Bürger dieser Republik gegenseitig achten können – und als wer wir von anderen anerkannt werden möchten. Dafür bildet die nationale Geschichte einen wichtigen Hintergrund. Nationale Überlieferungen und Mentalitäten, die Teil unserer Person geworden sind, reichen nämlich weit hinter die Anfänge dieser Republik zurück. Diese Verbindung aus politischem Selbstverständnis und historischem Bewußtsein bestimmt auch die Perspektive, aus der Goldhagens Buch für uns relevant wird. Weil aus der Mitte unseres Lebenszusammenhanges jenes singuläre Verbrechen hervorgegangen ist, an dem sich erst der Begriff eines „Verbrechens gegen die Menschheit" hat bilden können, stellen sich für die Nachgeborenen, die sich über ihre politische Existenz in diesem Lande klar werden wollen, wie von selbst die folgenden Fragen: Kann politische Massenkriminalität überhaupt einzelnen Personen oder Personengruppen zur Last gelegt werden? Wer waren gegebenenfalls die verantwortlich Handelnden, und was waren ihre Gründe? Waren normative Rechtfertigungsgründe, soweit sie den Ausschlag gegeben haben sollten, in Kultur und Denkweise verankert?

Es muß unser Selbstverständnis affizieren, wenn Goldhagen einem repräsentativen Kreis von irgendwie doch überzeugten Tätern eine subjektive Rechtfertigung zuschreibt, die ein integraler Bestandteil damals herrschender Grundüberzeugungen gewesen ist: „Die Juden repräsentierten für die Deutschen eine Art Riß im deutschen kulturellen Gewebe … einen Riß, an dem alle kulturellen Tabus zerbrachen, wenn die Deutschen sich über die Juden erregten."[1] Vorausgesetzt, daß die jeweils lebenden Generationen in der

1 Daniel Goldhagen, Hitlers willige Vollstrecker, Berlin 1996, S.87 (Seitenangaben im Text beziehen sich auf diese Ausgabe).

self-understanding. Present and past generations are bound up with one another, in their forms of thinking and feeling, their gestures and expressions, and in their ways of seeing, in a tapestry composed of countless cultural threads. To the extent to which it is legitimate, an assertion such as this must shake any naive trust in our own traditions. This critical attitude toward what is most our own is precisely what Goldhagen's study demands – and what calls forth the concern of some conservatives.

These conservative circles believe that only unquestioned traditions and strong values make a people "able for the future." Hence each and every skeptically probing backward look at tradition falls under the suspicion of being another instance of unbridled moralizing. Since 1989, a new sort of patriotic spirit has strengthened in the unified Germany, a spirit that regards the learning processes of the last forty years as already having gone "too far." On June 19 1948, Carl Schmitt noted that a "repentance preacher" like Karl Jaspers was beneath attention. The wretched vocabulary of repression audible in this indescribable "glossary", which registers every word of self-criticism as a "false eagerness to repent", was later reconstructed in Weikersheim; today it continues to exert its influence far beyond the circle of the incorrigible, in the wake of successful diversionary tactics against "political correctness." Even those who think differently than these hard-core conservatives seem to worry that Goldhagen's study will provoke a dubious moral judgment of the "unknowing" contemporaries of the Holocaust. And yet it is just this study that can serve as an illustration of how historical problems of subjective accountability bear an entirely distinct status once they enter the contemporary context of an ethical-political process of self-understanding. I will first recall the general sense in which a public use of history can be legitimate, and then go on to explain why Goldhagen's case histories are well-suited for an ethical-political process of self-understanding free from moralistic misunderstandings.

I

Modern historiography addresses itself to two different audiences: the guild of professional historians and the general reading public. A good work of

Art ihres Denkens und Empfindens, in der Gestik des Ausdrucks und in der Weise ihrer Wahrnehmung über ein Gespinst kultureller Fäden mit Lebensform und Denkweise vergangener Generationen verknüpft sind, muß eine solche Behauptung, wenn und soweit sie zutrifft, den naiven Vertrauensvorschuß gegenüber eigenen Traditionen erschüttern. Diese kritische Einstellung gegenüber Eigenem ist es, was Goldhagens Studie fördert – und was die Besorgnis mancher Konservativer auf den Plan ruft.

In diesen Kreisen glaubt man, daß nur fraglose Traditionen und starke Werte ein Volk „zukunftsfähig" machen. Deshalb gerät jeder skeptisch sondierende Rückblick in den Verdacht hemmungsloser Moralisierung. Seit 1989 festigt sich im vereinigten Deutschland eine neue Sorte von vaterländischem Geist, dem die Lernprozesse der letzten Jahrzehnte schon „zu weit" gehen. Am 19.6.48 notierte Carl Schmitt, daß ein „Bußprediger" wie Karl Jaspers kein Interesse verdiene. Das jämmerliche Verdrängungsvokabular jenes unsäglichen „Glossariums", das sich bei jedem selbstkritischen Wort gegen „falsche Bußwilligkeit" aufbäumt, ist später in Weikersheim wieder aufbereitet worden und wirkt heute, im Sog des erfolgreichen Ablenkungsmanövers gegen 'political correctness', weit über den Kreis der Unbelehrbaren hinaus. Auch Andersgesinnte scheinen zu fürchten, daß Goldhagens Studie eine fragwürdige moralische Abrechnung mit den „unwissenden" Zeitgenossen des Holocaust schürt. Gerade an dieser Untersuchung läßt sich jedoch zeigen, daß historische Fragen der subjektiven Zurechnung im aktuellen Zusammenhang einer ethisch-politischen Selbstverständigung einen ganz anderen Stellenwert haben. Ich werde zunächst daran erinnern, wie ein legitimer öffentlicher Gebrauch der Historie überhaupt möglich ist, um dann zu erklären, warum sich Goldhagens Fallstudien für eine von moralistischen Mißverständnissen freie ethisch-politische Selbstverständigung eignen.

I

Die moderne Geschichtsschreibung hat zwei Adressaten, die Zunft der Historiker und das allgemeine Publikum. Eine gute zeithistorische Darstellung

contemporary history should simultaneously satisfy both the critical standards of the profession, and the expectations of an interested public. Of course the view of the historian must not be directed by the interests of readers, who come to the historical text in search of explanations of their own historical position. The moment that the analytic perspective of the observer blurs with the perspective assumed by participants in a discourse of collective self-understanding, historiographical science degenerates into the politics of history. The union of historicism and nationalism once arose from just this confusion; a similar confusion is reflected today in tendencies that attempt to continue the cold war with historiographic means. It goes without saying that only historians of integrity, who insist upon the difference between observer and participant perspectives, are capable of being reliable experts.

Political criminal justice, for example, depends on historical experts. In cases of mass political criminality, both jurisprudence and contemporary historiography deal with the same questions of accountability. Both take an interest in who participated in crimes, whether the responsibility for the consequences of criminal actions should be borne by persons or ascribed to circumstances; whether those involved could have acted differently; whether in a given case they acted on the basis of normative convictions or out of self-interest; whether another choice of behavior could reasonably have been expected of them, and so forth. But the criminal justice can only benefit from historical documentation – just as, conversely, the historian can only benefit from the official proceedings of the office of the public prosecutor – as long as both, justice and historian, view the same phenomenon from different perspectives. The one side is interested in the question of the culpability for an act; the other in the explanation of its cause. From the historian's perspective, accountability for actions is not resolved in terms of guilt or innocence, but in terms of what kind of explanatory grounds exist. However that explanation will look – whether the causes lie predominantly in persons or in circumstances – a causal explanation can neither condemn nor excuse the actors. Only from the perspective of participants, who now encounter one another whether in a court of law or on the street, and call each other

soll gleichzeitig den kritischen Maßtäben der Wissenschaft und den Erwartungen einer interessierten Leserschaft gerecht werden. Vom Interesse dieser Leser, die Aufklärung über den eigenen historischen Standort heischen, darf sich freilich der Blick des Historikers nicht dirigieren lassen. Sobald die Sicht des analysierenden Beobachters mit der Perspektive verschmilzt, die die Teilnehmer an Selbstverständigungsdiskursen einnehmen, degeneriert Geschichtswissenschaft zu Geschichtspolitik. Das Bündnis von Historismus und Nationalismus hat sich einst dieser Konfusion verdankt; eine ähnliche Konfusion spiegelt sich heute noch in Tendenzen, den kalten Krieg mit historiographischen Mitteln fortzusetzen. Es versteht sich von selbst, daß nur integre Wissenschaftler, die in dieser Hinsicht auf der Differenz von Beobachter- und Teilnehmerperspektive beharren, zuverlässige Experten sein können.

Auf historische Experten ist beispielsweise die politische Strafjustiz angewiesen. Wenn es um politische Massenkriminalität geht, behandeln beide, Justiz und Zeitgeschichte, dieselben Zurechnungsfragen. Beide interessieren sich dafür, wer an solchen Verbrechen beteiligt war, ob die eingetretenen Handlungsfolgen eher den Personen oder eher den Umständen zur Last gelegt werden müssen, ob die verstrickten Personen überhaupt anders hätten handeln können, ob sie gegebenenfalls aus normativen Überzeugungen oder aus Klugheitsgründen gehandelt haben, ob ein anderes Verhalten zumutbar war usw. Aber der Strafrichter kann von historischen Gutachten – wie umgekehrt auch der Historiker von den Ermittlungsakten der Staatsanwaltschaft – nur profitieren, solange beide dieselben Phänomene aus verschiedenen Perspektiven betrachten. Die eine Seite ist an der Frage der Vorwerfbarkeit von Handlungen interessiert, die andere Seite an der Aufklärung ihrer Ursachen. Aus der Sicht des Historikers entscheidet die Zurechenbarkeit von Handlungen nicht über Schuld und Unschuld, sondern über die Art der erklärenden Gründe. Wie immer auch die Erklärung aussehen mag – ob die Gründe eher in den Personen oder in den Umständen liegen – als solche kann eine kausale Erklärung den Handelnden weder belasten noch entschuldigen. Erst aus der Perspektive von Beteiligten, die sich vor Gericht oder im Alltag begegnen und voneinander Rechenschaft

to account for themselves, do questions of accountability transform themselves into legal – or moral – questions.

The moral point of view also concerns the judgment of justice or injustice, although of course without the strict rules of procedure of a criminal proceeding. Historical knowledge can be put to use for moral controversies that take place in the context of the everyday just as much as for the ends of jurisprudence – as for example in the proverbial conflict between "fathers and sons." In both cases, historical knowledge becomes relevant in the same regard for those affected. However, this *view to justice* differs sharply from that point of view from which members of a current generation seek to secure for themselves a historical heritage which they, as citizens and members of a collective political life, must inherit in one way or another. It is this difference that concerns me. From the point of view of the ethical-political processes of self-understanding of citizens, the explanatory accounts of the historian have a different function than they would have in moral or legal discourses.

Here, in an ethical-political discourse, the question is not primarily the guilt or innocence of the forefathers but rather the critical self-assurance of their descendants. The public interest of those born later, who cannot know how they themselves would have acted, directs itself toward a different goal than the zealous moral judgments of the contemporaries of the Nazi years, who find themselves in the same context of interaction and demand a moral reckoning from each other. Painful revelations of the conduct of one's own parents and grandparents can only be an occasion for sorrow; they remain a private affair between those intimately involved. On the other hand, the later generations, as citizens, take a public interest in the darkest chapter of their national history regarding themselves – and in relation to the victims and their own descendants. They are not pointing a finger of blame at anyone else. They are trying to bring about some clarity concerning the cultural matrix of a burdened inheritance, to recognize what they themselves are collectively liable for; and what is to be continued, and what revised, from out of those traditions that earlier had formed such a disastrous motivational background. An awareness of collective liability emerges from widespread individually guilty conduct in the past.

fordern, verwandeln sich Fragen der Zurechnung in rechtliche – oder auch moralische – Fragen.

Denn auch unter moralischen Gesichtspunkten geht es, allerdings ohne die strikten Verfahrensregeln der Strafprozeßordnung, um die Beurteilung von Recht und Unrecht. Wie für die Zwecke der Justiz, so können historische Kenntnisse im Alltag natürlich auch für moralische Auseinandersetzungen verwendet werden – etwa in der sprichwörtlichen Auseinandersetzung zwischen „Vätern und Söhnen". In beiden Fällen wird historisches Wissen für die Betroffenen in der gleichen Hinsicht relevant. Diese Hinsicht auf Gerechtigkeit unterscheidet sich aber von jenem Aspekt, unter dem sich nachgeborene Generationen einer geschichtlichen Erbschaft vergewissern, die sie als Bürger eines politischen Gemeinwesens so oder so antreten müssen. Auf diese Differenz kommt es mir an. Die erklärenden Zurechnungen des Historikers gewinnen aus der Sicht der ethisch-politischen Selbstverständigung der Bürger eine andere Funktion, als sie in moralischen oder rechtlichen Diskursen haben würden.

Hier geht es nicht primär um Schuld oder Entschuldigung der Vorfahren, sondern um eine kritische Selbstvergewisserung der Nachkommen. Das öffentliche Interesse der später Geborenen, die nicht wissen können, wie sie selbst sich damals verhalten hätten, richtet sich auf ein anderes Ziel als der Eifer moralisch urteilender Zeitgenossen, die sich in demselben Interaktionszusammenhang vorfinden und einander zur Rede stellen. Schmerzliche Enthüllungen über das Verhalten der eigenen Eltern und Großeltern, die ja nur Trauer auslösen könnten, bleiben eine private Angelegenheit zwischen den unmittelbar Beteiligten. Als Bürger nehmen hingegen die Nachfahren ein öffentliches Interesse am dunkelsten Kapitel ihrer nationalen Geschichte im Hinblick auf sich selbst – und im Hinblick auf ihr Verhältnis zu den Opfern oder deren Nachkommen. Dabei zeigen sie nicht auf andere. Sie wollen sich über die kulturelle Matrix eines belastenden Erbes Klarheit verschaffen, um zu erkennen, wofür sie gemeinsam haften und was gegebenenfalls von den Traditionen, die damals einen verhängnisvollen Motivationshintergrund gebildet haben, noch fortwirkt und der Revision bedarf. Aus einem weit verbreiteten individuell schuldhaften Verhalten in der Vergangenheit entsteht das Bewußtsein kollektiver Haftung; mit der Zuschreibung

This has nothing to do with the ascription of collective guilt, a notion that is simply incoherent on conceptual grounds alone.[2]

II

Goldhagen's case histories, particularly his studies of police battalions and death marches, are intended to lead to conclusions, within a particular theoretical frame, that refer observed modes of behavior to orienting interpretive patterns and mentalities. The studies read like retrospectively conducted experiments, and in this sense conform to the standards of autonomous research. At the same time, however, the analytical perspectives encompassing the responsible perpetrators, the motivational grounds for their extraordinary actions, and the fundamental cognitive patterns that generated them, meet the public interest in a forthright, non-moralizing self-understanding that we have, in the land of the perpetrators. A clear strategy for analysis does not of course decide on the correctness of its results. But in the meantime, a number of professional controversies over the details of Goldhagen's work have been helpful in de-dramatizing its reception. Specialists familiar with the historical material have raised a host of objections concerning specific details, while taking Goldhagen's approach seriously.[3]

I myself am won over by the clear argumentative strategy. Goldhagen defines the circle of perpetrators he is investigating as constituted by membership in the institutions of murder, and direct participation in the operations of killing of Jews. These perpetrators may be said to stand at the end of a complex chain of events. Defining the perpetrators in this way solves by implication questions of objective accountability, which are far from easy to decide with re-

2 Herbert Jäger, who himself published an early study of criminal violence in the Nazi regime, emphasizes that Goldhagen's book does not argue for a collective guilt, as he is often accused of doing, but rather that the book "reveals a massive individual guilt". "Die Widerlegung des funktionalistischen Täterbildes", *Mittelweg 36*, February/March 1997.

3 Dieter Pohl, "Die Holocaust-Forschung und Goldhagens Thesen", *Vierteljahreshefte für Zeitgeschichte*, 1997, 1-48.

kollektiver Schuld, die schon aus begrifflichen Gründen ein Unding ist, hat das nichts zu tun.[2]

II

Goldhagens Fallstudien, insbesondere die Untersuchungen über Polizeibataillone und Todesmärsche, sollen innerhalb eines bestimmten theoretischen Rahmens Schlüsse von beobachteten Handlungsweisen auf orientierende Deutungsmuster und Mentalitäten erlauben. Die sozialwissenschaftlich angelegten Untersuchungen lesen sich wie nachgestellte Experimente und gehorchen insofern dem Eigensinn autonomer Forschung. Zugleich kommen aber die analytischen Gesichtspunkte, unter denen die verantwortlichen Täter, die Beweggründe ihrer exzeptionellen Handlungen und die zugrundeliegenden kognitiven Muster erfaßt werden, jenem öffentlichen Interesse entgegen, das wir, im Lande der Täter, an einer aufrichtigen, d.h. nicht-moralisierenden Selbstverständigung haben. Gewiß, eine klare Analysestrategie entscheidet noch nicht über die Richtigkeit der Ergebnisse. Aber inzwischen hat eine wohltuend entdramatisierende Auseinandersetzung der Fachleute mit den Details dieser Untersuchungen eingesetzt. Die mit dem Material vertrauten Spezialisten erheben im einzelnen eine Fülle von Einwänden, nehmen aber Goldhagens Ansatz ernst.[3]

Mich besticht das klare Argumentationsmuster. Goldhagen definiert den Kreis von Tätern, den er untersucht, durch die Zugehörigkeit zu Mordinstitutionen und die unmittelbare Teilnahme an Aktionen der Judenvernichtung. Diese Täter operieren gleichsam am Ausgang einer komplexen Geschehenskette. Dadurch erledigen sich Fragen der objektiven Zurechnung, die bei den stärker anonymen, arbeitsteiligen und administrativen Abläufen

2 Herbert Jäger, der selbst eine frühe Studie zur nationalsozialistischen Gewaltkriminalität vorgelegt hat, betont, daß Goldhagens Buch nicht, wie ihm oft vorgeworfen wird, eine Kollektivschuld behauptet, sondern „eine massenweise individuelle Schuld vor Augen führt“: Die Widerlegung des funktionalistischen Täterbildes, in: „Mittelweg 36“, Febr./März 1997.

3 Dieter Pohl, Die Holocaust-Forschung und Goldhagens Thesen, in: „Vierteljahreshefte für Zeitgeschichte“, 1/1997.

gard to the highly anonymous, differentiated and administrative execution of organized mass murder. At the same time, other questions – which norms were violated, and whether the perpetrators had knowledge of them – are settled by simple reference to the form of the crime itself. The analysis proper then starts with the question of whether the perpetrators acted in a subjectively accountable manner, whether they were aware of, and desired, the foreseeable and avoidable consequences of their actions. From the logic of everyday situations both within and outside of the murderous "service" itself, Goldhagen infers that the perpetrators must have had enough latitude for a reflective relation to their own action and involvement: "the perpetrators lived in a world in which reflection, discussion, and disagreement were possible."

This leads Goldhagen to probe the question of what ought reasonably to have been expected of the perpetrators: given the circumstances, did they have no choice but to act in the way that they did? Here Goldhagen points to killing operations that were manned by volunteers, or which perpetrators undertook on their own initiative; to declined offers to voluntarily excuse themselves from participation in massacres, and opportunities on the scene to refrain from taking part in killing operations without the threat of punishment. Supposedly, the men also understood that they could, if nothing else helped, urge to be transferred to another position, and that they could even refuse to follow orders without placing their own lives in danger. "Superfluous" violence, or the excessively gruesome nature of the killing operations (which Goldhagen describes for analytical reasons) also speaks against the assumption that the perpetrators found themselves trapped in a state of coercion. Goldhagen believes that he can rule out other possible grounds for excusing the perpetrators, such as the social-psychological effects of group pressure, a habituation to state-sanctioned mass criminality, or an unconscious attachment to state authority. There is a natural suspicion that this type of perpetrator may have been unusually fixated on the authority of his superior officers; Goldhagen refutes this too by pointing out instances of opposition and open subordination in other situations having nothing to do with the murder of Jews. Nor does self-interest seem to have been a decisive motivation. In any case, the proposition that corruption, ambition or interest in professional advancement played no decisive motivational role is important for Goldhagen's argument; one confirmation

des organisierten Massenmordes nicht so leicht zu entscheiden sind. Zugleich beantworten sich weitere Fragen – welche Normen verletzt worden sind und ob die Täter Kenntnis davon hatten – durch die Art der Verbrechen von selbst. Die Analyse setzt dann mit der Frage ein, ob die Täter subjektiv zurechenbar gehandelt haben, ob sie also die vorhersehbaren und vermeidbaren Folgen ihres Handelns gekannt und gewollt haben. Goldhagen schließt aus der Logik alltäglicher Situationen innerhalb wie außerhalb des mörderischen „Dienstes" auf den Spielraum, den die Beteiligten für eine reflektierte Stellungnahme zu ihren eigenen Handlungen und Verwicklungen gehabt haben müssen: „die Täter lebten in einer Welt, in der Nachdenklichkeit, Diskussion und Auseinandersetzung möglich waren." (S.318)

Sodann prüft Goldhagen Fragen der Zumutbarkeit: Haben nicht die Umstände ein anderes Verhalten unmöglich gemacht? Hier verweist er auf Aktionen, für die sich Freiwillige fanden oder welche die Männer aus eigener Initiative unternahmen; auf Angebote, sich von der Teilnahme an den Massakern freistellen zu lassen; und auf Gelegenheiten, sich in actu den Tötungsaktionen straflos zu entziehen. Offenbar wußten die Männer auch, daß sie sich notfalls versetzen lassen und sogar Befehle ohne Gefahr für Leib und Leben verweigern konnten. Ebensowenig spricht die „überflüssige" Gewalt, also die exzessive Grausamkeit der Mordeinsätze (auf die Goldhagen aus analytischen Gründen eingeht) für eine unentrinnbare Zwangslage. Andere Entschuldigungsgründe wie den sozialpsychologisch wirksamen Druck der Gruppe, die Gewöhnung an staatlich sanktionierte Massenkriminalität oder eine unbewußte Bindung an staatliche Autorität glaubt Goldhagen ausschließen zu können. Der naheliegenden Vermutung, daß dieser Typ von Tätern an die formale Autorität von Vorgesetzten in besonderer Weise fixiert gewesen sein könnte, begegnet Goldhagen mit Beispielen von Opposition und offenem Widerspruch in anderen Fällen, die nichts mit der Ermordung von Juden zu tun hatten. Auch Eigeninteresse scheint nicht überwiegend im Spiel gewesen zu sein. Für Goldhagens weitere Überlegung ist jedenfalls die Annahme wichtig, daß Korruption, Ehrgeiz oder Karriereinteresse nicht ausschlaggebend waren. Eine Bestätigung ist das geradezu bizarre Verhalten der Begleit-

for this assumption is the truly bizarre behavior of the teams of guards on the death marches during the final days of the war. If these people acted wilfully, without any drastic outward coercion or obvious inner compulsion; if they did not even act on utilitarian grounds, then we are forced to confront a picture of perpetrators who lacked the awareness that they were committing an injustice.

Philosophically, Goldhagen's study is inspired by the idea that evil is not to be understood as sheer aggression as such, but rather as the kind of aggression which the perpetrators believe themselves to be justified in committing. Evil is distorted good. With a wealth of details, from the absence of concern for secrecy to obscene sessions of posing for photographic mementoes, Goldhagen argues that many of the perpetrators must have regarded their murderous action as legitimate. But anyone who can appeal to his convictions in order to participate in an act that would count as criminal by any normal standard – indeed, in an act that must count as the monstrous itself – must have some powerful normative basis to justify such a dramatic exception. Here Goldhagen naturally refers back to the conception of "the Jew." Since he is obliged to reconstruct the bases for the morally selective perception of the perpetrators from their manifest acts, he collects evidence for the sharply differential treatment of designated victims. The antisemitic syndrome expresses itself in the fact that, in comparable situations, Jews consistently met a worse fate than Poles, Russians, political prisoners, and others. The perpetrators behaved more cruelly towards Jews than towards their other victims. As the current discussion on the Berlin Holocaust memorial continues, anyone inclined to mock the wish of survivors for a memorial that differentiates between different victims should pause to remember who it was who first set up this "hierarchy of victim groups." Following this course, Goldhagen reaches his central contention: in the end, antisemitic conceptions explain the murderous actions of these perpetrators.

The concluding step of the argument is supported by a fact already suggested in the title of the exemplary study by Christopher Browning: the perpetrators were in fact "quite ordinary men."[4] Goldhagen sharpens this thesis toward "ordinary Germans": with the help of the usual statisti-

4 Christopher Browning, *Ordinary Men*, New York 1992.

mannschaften auf den Todesmärschen während der letzten Kriegstage. Wenn aber diese Leute vorsätzlich, ohne drastischen äußeren oder offensichtlichen inneren Zwang und nicht einmal aus Nützlichkeitserwägungen gehandelt haben, drängt sich das Bild von Tätern auf, die kein Unrechtsbewußtsein hatten.

Philosophisch gesehen, ist Goldhagens Untersuchung von einem Gedanken inspiriert: Böse ist nicht die schiere Aggression als solche, sondern die, zu der sich der Täter berechtigt glaubt. Das Böse ist das verkehrte Gute. Daß viele Täter ihr mörderisches Handeln für legitim gehalten haben müssen, stützt Goldhagen mit vielen Details – vom fehlenden Bemühen um Geheimhaltung bis zu obszönen Fototerminen. Wer aus Überzeugung an einer Praxis teilnimmt, die nach normalen Maßstäben als verbrecherisch, ja als schlechthin abscheulich gilt, muß aber starke normative Gründe haben, um derart dramatische Ausnahmen zu rechtfertigen. Naheliegenderweise rekurriert Goldhagen auf die Vorstellungen von „dem Juden". Da er die Gründe für die moralisch selektiven Wahrnehmungen aus dem manifesten Verhalten rekonstruieren muß, trägt er Evidenzen für eine unterschiedliche Behandlung der designierten Opfer zusammen. Das antisemitische Syndrom äußert sich darin, daß Juden in vergleichbaren Situationen regelmäßig ein noch schlimmeres Schicksal zu erleiden hatten als Polen, Russen, politische Gefangene usw. Gegenüber Juden verhielten sich die Täter noch bösartiger als gegenüber ihren anderen Opfern. Wer sich heute, anläßlich der Diskussion über das Berliner Holocaust-Denkmal, über den Wunsch der Hinterbliebenen nach einem differenzierenden Eingedenken mokiert, sollte sich daran erinnern, von wem diese „Hierarchie der Opfergruppen" eingerichtet worden ist. Auf diesem Weg gelangt Goldhagen zu der zentralen Behauptung, daß letztlich antisemitische Auffassungen die mörderische Praxis dieser Täter erklären.

Der abschließende Schritt der Argumentation stützt sich auf einen Umstand, der schon durch den Titel der vorbildlichen Untersuchung von Christopher Browning nahegelegt worden war: daß die Täter eben „ganz gewöhnliche Männer" gewesen sind.[4] Goldhagen spitzt diese These auf „ganz

4 Christopher R. Browning, Ordinary Men, New York 1992.

cal criteria, he documents that the composition of Police Battalion 101 was roughly representative of the male population of Germany at the time. Naturally, retrospectively determined data of this sort cannot simply be equated with data derived from public opinion research. This is why serious qualifications are needed before one treats this police battalion as a representative sample, and draws the conclusion "that millions of other Germans would have behaved no differently had they found themselves in the same situation." [22] In the present context, it should be emphasized that such a conclusion ought not to mislead us to the stigmatizing reproach that the Germans were a "nation of murderers"[5], or only "potential murderers." Such counterfactual moral accusations are meaningless. Face to face, moral reproach can relate only to concrete, factual actions or omissions. But Goldhagen's counterfactual moral reflections, which quite reasonably refer to the undisputed and widespread antisemitic dispositions of the German population during this historical period.

III

The question of the rootedness of antisemitism in German culture during this period transcends the boundaries of any case study. Goldhagen is obliged to expand the scope of his analysis, from the already considerable number of perpetrators to the vast number of those who were indirectly involved. From 1933 onward the Jewish population was systematically excluded from every sphere of German society, a process that was carried out in full public view. This would not have been possible without the silent complicity of broader strata of the German population. Referring to social elites, Goldhagen justly asks: "How many German churchmen in the 1930s did not believe that the Jews were pernicious? ... How many generals ... did not want to cleanse Germany of the Jews? ...

5 Julius H. Schoeps, "Ein Volk von Mördern?", Hamburg 1996.

gewöhnliche Deutsche" zu. Er belegt anhand der üblichen sozialstatistischen Merkmale, daß die Zusammensetzung des Polizeibataillons 101 für die zeitgenössische männliche Bevölkerung in Deutschland annähernd repräsentativ gewesen ist. Natürlich können die retrospektiv ermittelten Daten nicht ohne weiteres mit Daten der Umfrageforschung gleichgesetzt werden. Deshalb sind erhebliche Qualifikationen angebracht, wenn man dieses Polizeibataillon wie ein repräsentatives Sample behandelt und den Schluß zieht, „daß auch Millionen anderer Deutscher nicht anders gehandelt hätten, wären sie in die entsprechenden Positionen gelangt" (S.22). In unserem Zusammenhang ist hervorzuheben, daß ein solcher Schluß nicht zu dem stigmatisierenden Vorwurf verführen darf, die Deutschen seien „ein Volk von Mördern"[5] oder auch nur von „potentiellen Mördern" gewesen. Denn kontrafaktische moralische Vorwürfe sind sinnlos. Face to face können sich moralische Vorhaltungen nur auf faktisches Handeln oder Unterlassen beziehen. Etwas anderes ist Goldhagens kontrafaktische Überlegung, die in einem historischen Zusammenhang den guten Sinn hat, auf die unbestritten große Verbreitung von antisemitischen Dispositionen in der deutschen Bevölkerung jener Zeit hinzuweisen.

III

Die Frage der Verwurzelung des Antisemitismus in der zeitgenössischen deutschen Kultur sprengt die Grenzen der Fallstudien. Goldhagen muß den Blick von der erheblichen Zahl der Täter auf die große Zahl der indirekt Beteiligten erweitern. Die jüdische Bevölkerung ist seit 1933 Schritt für Schritt konsequent aus allen Lebensbereichen der deutschen Gesellschaft ausgeschaltet worden, und dieser Prozeß hat sich in aller Öffentlichkeit vollzogen. Das wäre ohne das stillschweigende Einverständnis breiter Schichten der Bevölkerung nicht möglich gewesen. Im Hinblick auf die Eliten fragt Goldhagen mit Recht: „Wieviele deutsche Kirchenmänner waren in den dreißiger Jahren nicht der Meinung, daß die Juden eine Gefahr seien? ... Wieviele Generäle ... wollten Deutschland nicht von den Juden säubern? ... Wieviele

5 Julius H. Schoeps, Ein Volk von Mördern?, Hamburg 1996.

How many jurists, how many in the medical community, how many in other professions held the ubiquitous, public antisemitism, with its hallucinatory elements, to be sheer nonsense? … To be sure, not all churchmen, generals, jurists and others wanted to exterminate the Jews. Some wanted to deport them, a few wanted to sterilize them, and some would have been content to deprive the Jews 'only' of fundamental rights. Nevertheless, underlying all of these views was an eliminationist ideal." [430] The only objection that comes to my mind is that Goldhagen forgot the German professors.

On the other hand, these facts are not sufficient to justify speaking of the extermination of the Jews as a "national project of the Germans." Goldhagen himself refers to the medium of "society's conversation," in which all of these eliminationst intentions had to be articulated. The intersubjective constitution and the dynamics of public communication require a more differentiated picture. Even under the asymmetrical conditions of dictatorship, beliefs gain credence only in competition with other beliefs; cognitive models only against other cognitive models. But the objections of professional historians focus in the first place on the polemical thesis of a "direct road to Auschwitz."[425] The impression that Goldhagen's intentionalist argument overextends the credit of his empirical work by drawing global explanations from it can be countered by Goldhagen himself, who firmly refuses monocausal explanations and insists on a comparative approach. Goldhagen of course understands that in finding explanations for the Holocaust, one "[cannot] limit one's self to antisemitism alone, but [must] deal with countless other factors." [8] As a non-historian who has familiarized himself with the range of controversies in the broad field of Nazi research, I got anyway the impression that competing interpretive approaches tend to complement rather than contradict one another.

But it is not for me to offer a professional judgment on these matters. On the present occasion, we are evaluating the contributions that an American, a Jewish historian has made toward Germans' search for the proper way to come to terms with a criminal period of their history. In conclusion I want to consider a proposal that the legal theorist Klaus

Juristen, wieviele Mediziner, wieviele Angehörige anderer akademischer Berufe hielten den allgegenwärtigen, öffentlichen Antisemitismus mit seinen wahnhaften Zügen für schieren Unsinn? ...Sicherlich haben nicht alle Kirchenmänner, Generäle, Juristen und andere Führungskräfte die Vernichtung der Juden befürwortet. Einige wollten sie nur deportieren, andere wünschten deren Sterilisierung, wieder andere wollten den Juden ‚nur' ihre Grundrechte nehmen. Aber auch solchen Ansichten liegt eine eliminatorische Idealvorstellung zugrunde."(S.503) Dagegen läßt sich allenfalls einwenden, daß Goldhagen die deutschen Professoren vergessen hat.

Andererseits rechtfertigen diese Tatsachen nicht die Rede von der Judenvernichtung als einem „nationalen Projekt der Deutschen". Goldhagen selbst weist auf das Medium des „gesellschaftlichen Gesprächs" hin, in dem sich die eliminatorischen Absichten artikulieren mußten. Schon die intersubjektive Verfassung und die Dynamik öffentlicher Kommunikation verlangen ein differenziertes Bild. Auch unter den asymmetrischen Bedingungen einer Diktatur gelangen Meinungen nur gegen konkurrierende Meinungen, kognitive Modelle nur gegen andere Modelle zur Herrschaft. Der Streit der Historiker entzündet sich aber vor allem an der polemischen These eines „geraden Wegs nach Auschwitz" (S.497). Gegen diesen Goldhagen, der den Kredit seiner empirischen Untersuchungen intentionalistisch zu überziehen und daraus einen globalen Erklärungsanspruch abzuleiten scheint, kann man Goldhagen selbst ins Feld führen – den, der sich entschieden gegen monokausale Ansätze wehrt, der sich für ein komparatives Vorgehen stark macht und natürlich weiß, daß man sich für die Erklärung des Holocaust „nicht allein auf den Antisemitismus beschränken (kann), sondern auf zahlreiche weitere Faktoren ebenfalls eingehen (muß)" (S.8). Wer sich als Nicht-Historiker über die Kontroversen auf dem breiten Feld der NS-Forschung informiert, gewinnt ohnehin den Eindruck, daß sich die konkurrierenden Ansätze eher ergänzen als einander ausschließen.

Aber in diesen Dingen steht mir ein fachliches Urteil nicht zu. Was wir aus dem heutigen Anlaß zu beurteilen haben, sind Verdienste, die sich ein amerikanischer, ein jüdischer Historiker um den richtigen Umgang der Deutschen mit einem kriminellen Abschnitt ihrer Geschichte erworben hat. Ich will zum Schluß eine Überlegung aufgreifen, die ein juristischer Kollege, Klaus

Günther has made for the problem of how to cope in public with the history of political crimes. How we decide questions of accountability for crimes does not only depend on the facts, but also on how we view the facts. How much responsibility we ascribe to persons and how much to historical circumstances, where we draw the boundaries between individual freedom and constraint, guilt and innocence – these decisions depend on the particular pre-understanding with which we approach the events. The hermeneutic ability to recognize the true scope of responsibility and complicity for crime varies with our understanding of freedom: how we value ourselves as persons, and how much we expect from ourselves as political actors. An ethical-political discourse of collective self-understanding raises just this pre-understanding as a topic of discussion. How we see the distribution of guilt and innocence in the past also reflects the present norms according to which we are willing to accord one another mutual respect as citizens of this Republic. And historians who participate in this discourse do so no longer as experts, but, like us, in the role of intellectuals.

Here is where I see Goldhagen's real contribution. He is not arguing for supposed anthropological universals or regularities to which all persons are equally subjected. Such regularities may well serve to explain a portion of the unspeakable, as some comparative research in genocide maintains. Goldhagen's work, however, refers to very specific traditions and mentalities, to ways of thinking and perceiving that belong to a particular cultural context – not something unalterable to which we have been consigned by fate, but factors that can be transformed through a change of consciousness, and which in the meantime have actually been transformed through political enlightenment. The union of anthropological pessimism and a fatalistic kind of historicism in this country is in fact a part of the very problem whose solution it pretends to offer. Daniel Goldhagen deserves our thanks for strengthening our ability to take another view of the past.

Translation by Max Pensky

Günther, allgemein zum öffentlichen Umgang mit der Geschichte politischer Kriminalität angestellt hat. Offenbar hängt es nicht nur von den Tatsachen, sondern auch von unserem Blick auf die Tatsachen ab, wie wir Fragen der Zurechnung entscheiden. Welche Anteile wir im historischen Rückblick den Personen, welche den Umständen zuschreiben, wo wir die Grenze zwischen Freiheit und Zwang, Schuld und Entschuldigung ziehen, hängt auch von einem Vorverständnis ab, mit dem wir an das Geschehen herantreten. Die hermeneutische Bereitschaft, den wahren Umfang von Verantwortung und Mitwissen anzuerkennen, variiert mit unserem Verständnis von Freiheit – wie wir uns als verantwortliche Personen einschätzen und wieviel wir uns selbst als politisch Handelnden zumuten. Mit Fragen der ethisch-politischen Selbstverständigung steht dieses Vorverständnis selbst zur Diskussion. Wie wir Schuld und Unschuld im historischen Rückblick verteilt sehen, spiegelt auch die Normen, nach denen wir uns gegenseitig als Bürger dieser Republik zu achten willens sind. An diesem Diskurs nehmen übrigens die Historiker nicht mehr als Experten, sondern wie wir anderen in der Rolle von Intellektuellen teil.

Hier sehe ich Goldhagens eigentliches Verdienst. Er richtet den Blick nicht auf unterstellte anthropologische Universalien, nicht auf Gesetzmäßigkeiten, denen präsumtiv alle Menschen unterworfen sind. Die mögen, wie die vergleichende Genozidforschung behauptet, auch einen Teil des Unsäglichen erklären. Goldhagens Erklärung bezieht sich jedoch auf spezifische Überlieferungen und Mentalitäten, auf Denk- und Wahrnehmungsweisen eines bestimmten kulturellen Kontextes. Sie bezieht sich nicht auf ein Unveränderliches, in das wir uns zu schicken haben, sondern auf Faktoren, die durch einen Bewußtseinswandel verändert werden können – und die sich inzwischen auch durch politische Aufklärung verändert haben. Der anthropologische Pessimismus, der hierzulande mit einem fatalistischen Historismus im Bunde steht, ist eher Teil des Problems, dessen Lösung er zu liefern vorgibt. Daniel Goldhagen gebührt Dank dafür, daß er uns in einem anderen Blick auf die Vergangenheit bestärkt hat.

Jan Philipp Reemtsma

Turning Away from Denial

Hitler's Willing Executioners as a Counterforce to "Historical Explanation"

A book and its effect – that is to be the subject addressed here, not the legend about a book, not the presumed imputation of collective guilt or the alleged assertion of some immutable national character – nor, dear Daniel Goldhagen, is the subject to be something we promised one another in New York a few weeks ago: that the discussion might finally turn to issues of true disagreement. My subject is to be the success of a book in Germany, a success that is not only worth our remarking it, but also curiously remarkable. As foolish as it is, of course, to trace the book's success, as has happened here and there, to the charm of its author (though I would not wish in any way to dispute that charm), at the very least it takes more than mere quality to make a bestseller. A bestseller supplies a commodity that satisfies a preexistent demand – and of what did that demand consist?

When "Schindler's List" proved a success, the film's critics wanted to see it as the acceptance of an offer of exculpation. But they were wrong. Those who saw the film were concerned not with the "good German" who had at last been discovered, but rather with the issue of individual responsibility – or put another way, with individual freedom. When Daniel Goldhagen's book proved a success, it was occasionally regarded as connected with or as a successor to that film, and at times that was meant as a reproach. Unfairly so, I would say. One of the consequences of the years 1933–45 can be seen in the curious conception of freedom that became popular here in Germany, a conception that revealed itself very

Jan Philipp Reemtsma

Abkehr vom Wunsch nach Verleugnung

Über „Hitlers willige Vollstrecker" als Gegenstück zur „historischen Erklärung"

Von einem Buch und seiner Wirkung soll die Rede sein, nicht mehr von der Legende über ein Buch, vom angeblichen Vorwurf der Kollektivschuld und der Behauptung eines unabänderlichen Nationalcharakters – auch nicht von dem, lieber Daniel Goldhagen, was wir einander vor wenigen Wochen in New York versprochen haben: daß es doch endlich einmal zur Diskussion der Differenzen kommen möge. Die Rede sei von dem Erfolg eines Buches in Deutschland, und der ist ja nicht nur bemerkenswert, sondern auch merkwürdig. So albern es natürlich ist, ihn auf, wie zuweilen geschehen, den Charme seines Verfassers zurückzuführen (womit ich den allerdings auch nicht in Abrede stellen möchte), so gehört wenigstens zu einem *Bestseller* doch mehr als bloße Qualität. Ein Bestseller ist ein Angebot, das eine bestehende Nachfrage befriedigt – worin bestand die?

Als „Schindlers Liste" ein Erfolg wurde, wollten die Kritiker dieses Films den als ein angenommenes Exkulpationsangebot verstehen. Sie hatten aber unrecht. Nicht der endlich einmal gefundene „gute Deutsche" war das, was diejenigen, die den Film sahen, beschäftigte, sondern das Thema der individuellen Verantwortung – anders gesagt, das der individuellen Freiheit. Als Daniel Goldhagens Buch ein Erfolg wurde, wurde es zuweilen in Nachbarschaft oder Nachfolge dieses Films gesehen, und manchmal war das als Einwand gemeint. Zu unrecht, wie ich finde. Man mag es als eine der Folgen der Jahre 1933-45 ansehen, daß ein merkwürdiges Verständnis von Freiheit hierzulande populär wurde, das sich immer dann sehr deutlich zeigte, wenn je-

clearly whenever someone was admonished that he or she apparently did not know what it means to live under a totalitarian regime. Individual freedom appeared to be something available in given quantities, and anyone who enjoined responsibility appeared to be someone proceeding from an inaccurate empirical assumption of a given quantum of freedom. As freedom vanished, so, too, did morality. The disquieting popularity of a rhetorical phrase such as, "I did it because someone else would have done it in any case," not only fails to recognize that morality begins with the question of what *I* am to do, and that there is most definitely a decisive difference between whether I or someone else does it, but it also makes a muddle of complicity in a deed and the possible inability to prevent it. The notion of a society in which there is only complicity and suicidal resistance, with nothing in between, is therefore not just a false picture of German society between 1933 and 1945, but also a false picture of human beings in – and here I shall be cautious – almost every society.

There is, however, something like an involuntary consensus between a mentality that insists on the disavowal of freedom and morality, and historiography. It may be that the Enlightenment's bias against that discipline originally had something to do with this fact. Even if in writing history one is, of course, not duty-bound by method to record why everything *had* to happen as it happened, the scope history can allow to the portrayal of an event as a matter of pure chance is as small as the scope it can give to rhetorical phrases such as "it happened because they wanted it that way." It is a question of genre. That kind of perception of reality lies outside historiography's jurisdiction. That means, however, that it has great difficulty with a mode of presentation systematically focused on making manifest the scope of latitude inherent in a given act. But in writing history, if someone suggests that a person could also have acted differently – a routine occurrence in courts of law, for instance, or in political discussion – that can easily appear to be an admission that one has not worked hard enough to discover why someone had to act as he or she did.

It is interesting to observe why, for this very reason, the discussion of Goldhagen's book as a "historians' debate" had to fail. Only a few weeks ago, I heard a well-known historian speak publicly about Goldhagen's the-

mandem vorgehalten wurde, er wisse wohl nicht, was es heiße, unter einem totalitären Regime zu leben. Individuelle Freiheit schien etwas zu sein, das in bestimmten Quantitäten vorhanden war, und derjenige, der Verantwortung einklagte, erschien als einer, der von einer unzutreffenden empirischen Annahme über ein bestimmtes Freiheitsquantum ausging. Mit der Freiheit verschwand die Moral. Die beunruhigende Popularität einer rhetorischen Figur wie der, man habe irgend etwas darum getan, weil es sonst ein anderer getan hätte, verkennt ja nicht nur, daß Moral mit der Frage beginnt, was denn *ich* tue, und daß sehr wohl ein ganz entscheidender Unterschied darin besteht, ob ich es tue oder ein anderer, sondern verwechselt auch Mittäterschaft und die mögliche Unfähigkeit, etwas zu verhindern. Das Bild einer Gesellschaft, in der es zwischen Mit*täterschaft* und selbstmörderischem Widerstand nichts gibt, ist dabei nicht nur ein falsches Bild der deutschen Gesellschaft zwischen 1933 und 45, sondern ein falsches Bild vom Menschen, in (ich will vorsichtig sein:) fast jeder Gesellschaft.

Nun gibt es etwas wie ein unfreiwilliges Einverständnis zwischen einer Mentalität, die auf Verleugnung von Freiheit und Moral besteht, und der Historiographie. Mag sein, daß das Ressentiment der Aufklärung gegen diese Disziplin ursprünglich damit zu tun hatte. Wenn auch natürlich Geschichtsschreibung nicht methodisch darauf verpflichtet ist, uns aufzuschreiben, warum alles so hat kommen *müssen*, wie es gekommen ist, so ist der Raum, den sie der Beschreibung eines Ereignisses als puren Zufalls einräumen kann, ebenso gering wie der, den sie rhetorischen Figuren wie „es geschah darum, weil sie es eben so hatten haben wollen" geben darf. Es ist eine Frage des Genres. Historiographie ist für solche Art der Wirklichkeitswahrnehmung nicht zuständig. Das bedeutet aber, daß sie sich schwer tut mit einer Darstellungsweise, die systematisch auf die Sichtbarmachung von Handlungsspielräumen gerichtet ist. Der Hinweis, jemand habe auch anders handeln können – vor Gericht etwa oder in der politischen Auseinandersetzung gang und gäbe –, wirkt in der Geschichtsschreibung leicht wie einer darauf, man habe noch nicht zureichend herausgearbeitet, warum er so habe handeln müssen, wie er es denn getan hat.

Es ist interessant zu sehen, wie bereits aus diesem Grund die Diskussion um Goldhagens Buch als *Historiker*debatte mißlingen mußte. Noch vor wenigen Wochen hörte ich einen bekannten Historiker öffentlich von Goldha-

sis that German anti-Semitism is genetically conditioned, revealing by that statement how foreign to him was the very idea that had actually been Goldhagen's chief concern: not to present human beings as acting on their opinions with no will of their own, but to insist that human beings are also responsible for what they believe to be right. And so on various podiums, historians accused Goldhagen of not sufficiently explaining his ideas, while Goldhagen demonstrated that the genre of "historical explanation" is not the only way in which to present historical material, and indeed is perhaps not even especially useful for some purposes.

It is indeed remarkable that it was always by an introductory statement that Goldhagen won over his audience, often simply leaving his fellow panelists in the wake: for every other great historical outrage, for every other mass killing or genocide, we assume that the murderers did what they did out of conviction in the justice of their actions – only with the Holocaust do we look for explanations that might make plausible why the Germans perpetrated, allowed, or intentionally overlooked something they fundamentally did not wish.[1] And indeed this notion is found not so much in grand theories, but in the rhetoric, in the details – when, for instance, one reads in the history of a company that its moral scruples against employing Jewish forced labor fell only after certain events had occurred, but without any documentation whatever that might prove the moral scruples of so much as a single person in the company's upper management.

It was not the apparent simplicity of Goldhagen's thesis that constituted its success over the more complex theories of the historians, but the abandonment of any wish for denial[2] – which had entered into the rhetoric even of historians who are above every political suspicion. I know it sounds somewhat old-fashioned for me to speak of a complementary wish for truth that is in fact capable of prevailing over the wish for denial. But from a psychological viewpoint, truth is so often the ob-

1 Cf. Daniel Goldhagen, Hitler's Willing Executioners. Ordinary Germans and the Holocaust (New York: 1996), p. 29.

2 To speak of a "wish to repress" is incorrect, even in a psychological sense.

gens These eines genetisch bedingten Antisemitismus der Deutschen sprechen, und er zeigte damit vor allem, wie fremd ihm der Gedanke blieb, um den es Goldhagen eigentlich gegangen war: Menschen nicht als willenlose Exekutoren ihrer Ansichten darzustellen, sondern zu betonen, daß Menschen auch für das verantwortlich sind, was sie für richtig halten. So hielten auf den Podien die Historiker Goldhagen vor, er erkläre nicht zureichend, während Goldhagen demonstrierte, daß das Genre „historische Erklärung" nicht die einzige Art und Weise sein muß, historisches Material aufzubereiten, und für manche Zwecke vielleicht sogar nicht besonders tauglich.

Bemerkenswert war ja, daß es immer ein Eingangsstatement gewesen ist, mit dem Goldhagen das Publikum gewann und seine Mitdiskutanten oft hinter sich ließ: bei jedem historischen Großverbrechen, bei jedem Massenmord oder Genozid gehen wir davon aus, daß die Mörder ihre Taten für gerechtfertigt oder geboten gehalten haben – nur beim Holocaust suchen wir nach Erklärungen, die plausibel machen sollen, warum die Deutschen einen Genozid begingen, duldeten oder geflissentlich übersahen, den sie im Grunde nicht wollten.[1] Tatsächlich findet sich diese Vorstellung gar nicht so sehr in den großen Theorien als vielmehr, in Rhetorik erstarrt, im Detail, wenn man etwa in einer Unternehmensgeschichte liest, die moralischen Barrieren gegen die Verwendung jüdischer Zwangsarbeiter seien nach dem Eintreten bestimmter Umstände gefallen, ohne daß eine Quelle angeführt wird, die etwa die moralischen Skrupel auch nur eines der Mitglieder der Geschäftsleitung belegte.

Nicht die scheinbare Einfachheit der These Goldhagens gegenüber den komplexeren Theorien der Historiker machten den Erfolg aus, sondern die Abkehr vom noch in die Rhetorik politisch vollkommen unverdächtiger Historiker eingegangenen Wunsch nach Verleugnung.[2] Ich weiß, daß es etwas altmodisch klingt, wenn ich vom komplementären Wunsch nach Wahrheit spreche, der sich gegen den nach Verleugnung doch durchzusetzen imstande ist. Aber psychologisch gesehen ist die Wahrheit ja gerade darum so oft das Objekt der Entstellung durch Wünsche, weil Wahrheit selbst ein kulturell so

1 Vgl. etwa Daniel Goldhagen, Hitlers willige Vollstrecker. Ganz normale Deutsche und der Holocaust, Berlin 1996, S.29.

2 Von „Verdrängung" zu sprechen ist nicht einmal im psychoanalytischen Sinne richtig.

ject of distortion by our wishes, because truth itself is such a culturally laden value. There are few social sectors in which the differentiation between true and false, between truth and lies is irrelevant. Where truth is itself morally laden, it is indeed not easy to live with lies. But this merely in passing. Of greater importance, is that the wish for denial and the wish for truth lay too close together. The outrage that mass killings could be committed in a country that considered itself civilized, and the desire to understand how that could have been possible, could no more be satisfied by historical research that gave little attention to how its perpetrators thought, than it could by research that concentrated solely on the society's elites. The fear of a study of the average man and the possibility of recognizing in him one's own grandfather, father, or uncle (or aunt, or mother) has finally been replaced by the willingness to take the risk of such a recognition.

This circumstance made three unexpected successes possible. The first is the Klemperer diaries, which, more than any text before them are closer to what German policies directed at Jews actually meant in normal everyday life, and are likewise a permanent reflection of the question of just how deep the consensus between regime and populace actually was in executing those policies. The second success is "War of Extermination. The Crime of the Wehrmacht, 1941–1944," an exhibition mounted by the Hamburg Institute for Social Research – and here, too, it is a matter of the average man, of the point of intersection between the regime and the general population, in this instance, the Wehrmacht. And third, then, Daniel Goldhagen's Hitler's Willing Executioners, subtitled Ordinary Germans and the Holocaust. The success of these two books and one exhibition show that there is a collective willingness to ask the question, and to accept the threefold answer, provided with a different accent each time: that the obsession of viewing Europe's Jewish population as a problem that had to be solved was extremely widespread and that both the formulation of this phantasmal problem and its possible solutions resulted in an increasingly murderous vocabulary – and that the circle of those willing to participate actively was far larger than had previously been assumed.

besetztes Gut ist. Wenige gesellschaftliche Sektoren, in denen die Unterscheidung von wahr und falsch und Wahrheit und Lüge belanglos ist. Wo Wahrheit selber moralisch besetzt ist, lebt es sich mit der Lüge tatsächlich nicht gut. Aber das nur nebenbei. Wichtiger noch, daß der Wunsch nach Verleugnung und der nach Wahrheit zu nahe beieinanderlagen. Das Entsetzen darüber, daß der Massenmord in einem Land, das sich selber für zivilisiert hielt, exekutiert werden konnte, und der Wunsch, zu verstehen, wie das hatte möglich werden können, konnte mit einer Geschichtsforschung, die den Denkweisen der Täter wenig Aufmerksamkeit schenkte, ebensowenig befriedigt werden, wie durch deren Konzentration auf gesellschaftliche Eliten. Die Furcht vor der Betrachtung des Jedermann und der Möglichkeit, in ihm den eigenen Großvater, Vater oder Onkel (oder die Tante und die Mutter) wiederzuerkennen, ist schließlich durch die Bereitschaft ersetzt worden, sich diesem Erkenntnisrisiko auszusetzen.

Dieser Umstand machte drei unerwartete Erfolge möglich. Der eine ist der der Klemperer-Tagebücher, die sowohl näher am ganz normalen Alltag der deutschen Judenpolitik waren als je ein Text zuvor, als auch eine permanente Reflexion der Frage sind, wie tief der Konsens von Regime und Bevölkerung in der Exekution dieser Politik tatsächlich gewesen ist. Der zweite Erfolg ist die Ausstellung „Vernichtungskrieg. Verbrechen der Wehrmacht 1941-1944" des Hamburger Instituts für Sozialforschung – auch hier geht es um eine Schnittstelle von Regime und Bevölkerung, die Wehrmacht, und um den Jedermann. Drittens eben Daniel Goldhagens „Hitlers willige Vollstrecker" mit dem Untertitel „Ganz gewöhnliche Deutsche und der Holocaust". Der Erfolg der beiden Bücher und der einen Ausstellung zeigt, daß eine kollektive Bereitschaft vorhanden ist, sich dieser Frage zu stellen, und die dreifach gegebene – jeweils unterschiedlich akzentuierte – Antwort zu akzeptieren: daß die Obsession, die jüdische Bevölkerung Europas als ein Problem zu sehen, das gelöst werden müsse, äußerst weit verbreitet gewesen ist und die Formulierung des Problemphantasmas sowie der möglichen Lösungen in einem zunehmend mörderischen Vokabular erfolgte – und daß der Kreis derjenigen, die zur Mittäterschaft bereit waren, weit größer war, als zuvor angenommen.

Evidence for an anti-Semitism in Germany and Austria that was both widespread and rightly termed eliminationist was not first found in Daniel Goldhagen's book, in the letters from the field published in conjunction with the exhibition, or in Klemperer's records of his conversations. In Karl Kraus's Last Days of Mankind, two men buying newspapers converse at the start of act four: "'And once the offensive starts, just watch – boom, and that's that!' – 'Then it's the Jews turn – wipe 'em out !'"[3] And in 1920, Kurt Tucholsky says of the graffiti on the toilets at the University of Rostock – "Jews out !" "Beat the Jews to death!" "Time for a pogrom!": "The writers of these inscriptions are our future judges, civil servants, prosecutors, priests …"[4] The question of why such evidence, even if it has not totally vanished perhaps from the consciousness of written history, has nevertheless been neglected with astonishing unanimity as the explanation for "how it could come to this," leads us to another factor shared in common by all three aforementioned successes from the years 1995–96: all three take as their theme that portion of the genocide that lies "before" Auschwitz, both temporally and in terms of its being prior to the impetus of escalation. Klemperer writes about the resentment and hatred, the system of regulations, and the Gestapo's terror, which was equally systematic, but also depended on the personal initiative and sadistic creativity of individuals; the Wehrmacht exhibition and Hitler's Willing Executioners deal with sectors of extermination policy outside the death camps.

One of the most important presuppositions in Daniel Goldhagen's book is the notion that fixating on the "really" hard thing to understand – that is, the mass killings, especially those that the equally popular and problematic metaphor terms "industrial" – ultimately hinders our understanding. What has taken place here, if I may put it that way, is a *exoneration by the extreme*. It was not there from the start, it is the result of a specifically German dynamic of denial.

3 Karl Kraus, Die letzten Tage der Menschheit (Munich: 1974), p. 428.

4 Kurt Tucholsky, Gesamtausgabe, vol. 4 (Reinbek: 1996), p. 277ff.

Die Belege für einen in Deutschland und Österreich weit verbreiteten und zu Recht eliminatorisch zu nennenden Antisemitismus haben sich nun allerdings nicht erst in Daniel Goldhagens Buch, den im Zusammenhang mit der Ausstellung publizierten Feldpostbriefen und Klemperers Mitschriften seiner Gespräche gefunden. In Karl Kraus' „Letzten Tagen der Menschheit" unterhalten sich zu Beginn des Vierten Aktes zwei Zeitungsleser: „‚Wenn jetzt die Offensive kommt, dann paß auf – rrtsch obidraht!' – ‚Und nachher mit die Juden – ramatama!'"[3] – 1920 schreibt Kurt Tucholsky über die Inschriften auf den Toiletten der Universität Rostock: „Juden raus!" „Haut die Juden tot!" „Man mache ein Pogrom!": „Die Inschriftenmacher sind unsere künftigen Richter, Beamten, Staatsanwälte, Priester..."[4] Die Frage, warum solche Belege aus dem Bewußtsein der Geschichtsschreibung vielleicht nicht verschwunden, aber doch mit erstaunlicher Einmütigkeit als für die Erklärung, „wie es denn dazu kommen konnte", vernachlässigenswert behandelt worden sind, führt auf eine weitere Gemeinsamkeit der drei genannten unvorhergesehenen Erfolge der Jahre 1995/96, den Umstand, daß alle drei den Teil des Genozids thematisieren, der „vor" Auschwitz liegt, einerseits zeitlich gesehen, andererseits von der Eskalationsdynamik her. Klemperer schreibt über Ressentiment und Haß, das Verordnungssystem und den ebenso systematischen wie sich auf persönliche Initiative und sadistische Kreativität des Einzelnen stützenden Terror der Gestapo, die Wehrmachtsausstellung und „Hitlers willige Vollstrecker" Sektoren der Vernichtungspolitik außerhalb der Vernichtungslager.

Eine der wichtigsten Voraussetzungen in Daniel Goldhagens Buch ist die Überlegung, daß die Fixierung auf das „eigentliche" Verstehensproblem, die Massentötungen, vor allem jene mit einer ebenso populären wie problematischen Metapher als „industriell" bezeichneten in den Vernichtungslagern, das Verstehen im Grunde behindere. Es findet hier, so möchte ich es formulieren, eine *Entlastung durch das Extrem* statt. Es gab sie nicht von Anfang an, sie ist ein Resultat der spezifisch deutschen Verleugnungsdynamik.

3 Karl Kraus, Die letzten Tage der Menschheit, München 1974, S.428

4 Kurt Tucholsky, Gesamtausgabe Band 4, Reinbek 1996, S.277ff.

In her biography of Albert Speer, Gitta Sereny writes about the family of Speer's liaison adjutant to the General Staff: "When I met the Posers I was already aware of what army people who served in Russia necessarily had to have known about the murders there. Not only because of the Komissar Befehl and the subsequent verbally transmitted orders told them, but because it was impossible not to either see what was being done or, at the very least (as was the case for many officers on the Chiefs of Staff), hear it described."[5] And Speer's attorney presents her with this remarkable statement: "'I, too, after all, knew in the 1930s that Jews were being badly treated, that they could no longer be judges or lawyers. And believe me, I often thanked God that I wasn't a Jew. I had Jewish friends and tried to help, and sometimes one could help. One knew it was miserable to be a Jew in Hitler's Germany, but one didn't know it was a catastrophe; one didn't know what happened to them. Until a day in 1943, when a client of mine who was a medic in Russia came back with photographs of executions of Jews, I knew absolutely nothing of this. I told him to burn or bury the photographs and to tell no one what he had seen. And I didn't tell anybody either, not even my wife. ... I don't think it was a secret that people were being executed; what we didn't know was that they were being systematically mass-murdered.'" And later, concerning the Nuremberg trials: "'Strangely ... although the shadow of extermination of the Jews hovered over the trial from beginning to end, it was not much discussed. ... You see, they had all these witnesses ... testifying to beatings and starvation in forced-labor and concentration camps. But somehow those horrors were, well, almost expected. ... Did you notice that even Dr. Gilbert in his book barely mentions the gas chambers? As if even he could not bear to pronounce the word.'"[6]

Such horrors – the photographs from Russia, the reports from the slave-labor and concentration camps – those were simply to be expected,

5 Gitta Sereny, Albert Speer: His Battle with Truth (New York: 1995), p. 458.

6 Ibid., p. 581ff.

In ihrer Speer-Biographie schreibt Gitta Sereny über die Familie des Speerschen Verbindungsoffiziers zum Generalstab: „Als ich die Posers kennenlernte, war mir bereits klar, daß Wehrmachtsangehörige, die den Rußlandkrieg mitgemacht hatten, von den Massakern dort unweigerlich erfahren haben mußten. Nicht nur, weil der Kommissarbefehl und die folgenden, mündlich übermittelten Befehle offen zum Mord aufriefen, sondern auch, weil es unmöglich war, nicht zu sehen, was geschah, oder nicht wenigstens (wie viele Offiziere des Generalstabs) davon zu hören."[5], und Speers Anwalt Flächsner macht ihr gegenüber dieses bemerkenswerte Statement: „es wurde mir ja schließlich in den dreißiger Jahren klar, daß es den Juden schlecht ging, daß sie nicht mehr Richter oder Anwälte sein durften. Und, glauben Sie mir, ich habe Gott oft gedankt, daß ich nicht Jude war. Ich hatte jüdische Freunde und versuchte, ihnen zu helfen; manchmal war das möglich. Man wußte, daß es gefährlich war, in Hitlerdeutschland Jude zu sein, aber man wußte nicht, daß es eine Katastrophe war. Ich wußte absolut nichts, bis eines Tages 1943 einer meiner Mandanten, der als Sanitäter in Rußland tätig war, mit Fotografien zurückkam, die Erschießungen von Juden zeigten. Ich riet ihm, sie zu verbrennen oder zu vergraben und niemandem zu sagen, was er gesehen hatte. Auch ich habe niemandem davon erzählt, nicht einmal meiner Frau. (...) Ich glaube nicht, daß es ein Geheimnis war, daß Menschen hingerichtet wurden. Was wir nicht wußten, war, daß ein systematischer Massenmord stattfand." Und später, über den Nürnberger Prozeß: „Seltsamerweise (...) lag der Schatten der Judenvernichtung zwar von Anfang bis Ende über dem Prozeß, doch kam das Thema nur selten zur Sprache. (...) Sehen Sie, man hatte alle diese Zeugen, die (...) von den Schlägen und vom Hunger in den Zwangsarbeiter- und Konzentrationslagern berichteten. Doch irgendwie, ja, erwartete man solche Greuel geradezu. (...) Haben Sie bemerkt, daß sogar Dr. Gilbert in seinem Buch die Gaskammern kaum erwähnt? Als ob er nicht einmal das Wort hätte aussprechen können."[6]

Solche Greuel – die Fotos aus Rußland, die Berichte aus den Arbeits- und Konzentrationslagern – erwartete man geradezu – nicht den systematischen

5 Gitta Sereny, Das Ringen mit der Wahrheit. Albert Speer und das deutsche Trauma, München 1995, S.531.

6 Ebd., S.671f.

but not systematic mass killing in camps built for that sole purpose, or, in the case of Auschwitz, in a city built for that sole purpose. Nowadays gas chambers and systematic mass killings are denied by only a minority, who are viewed as partly pathological, partly criminal, but talk of those horrors – and shortly after 1945, it was expected that they would indeed be spoken of – can still cause a scandal or two.[7]

Speer is moreover a key figure in this reversal. In Nuremberg he accepted responsibility for Auschwitz, and later admitted complicity in its crime – at the same time that he denied ever knowing any specific details. He should have known them, he admitted, and that made him an accomplice. And with that Speer had discovered a downright brilliant turn of phrase. It was a confession of shared responsibility – something demanded both of him and the German people – but it was more than that, it was a confession of guilt, individual guilt in fact, and yet, as everyone concurred, a confession that, especially at such a high level, almost ennobled him. Yes, a downright brilliant turn of phrase, one can say – in light of his intentional and demonstrable lies about the extent of what he not only knew but had also in fact seen – a turn of phrase that was as breathtakingly impudent[8] as it was thoroughly successful.

And if this division of the holocaust into two tidily detached operations – killing in the death camps by a murderous elite and killing as an ostensibly war-related act, executed by units in various kinds of uniforms – first led people to overlook the historical uniqueness of the death camps, and then to keep their eyes fixed only on them, it also resulted in an understanding of the dynamics of violence that remains inadequate even today. For the same holds true of both parts: "Ultimately the holocaust took place because at the most basic level individual human beings killed other human beings in large numbers over an extended period of time."[9] The systematic underestimation of anti-Semitism cannot be separated form this reality.

7 Cf. Sereny, op. cit., p. 333ff.

8 Cf. esp. Sereny, op. cit., pp. 585ff., 563ff.

9 Christopher Browning, Ordinary Men: Reserve Police Battalion 101 and the Final Solution in Poland (New York: 1992), p. xvii .

Massenmord in eigens dazu errichteten Lagern, oder, im Falle von Auschwitz, einer eigens dazu errichteten Stadt. Heute werden die Gaskammern und der systematische Massenmord nur von einer für teils pathologisch, teils kriminell angesehenen Minderheit geleugnet, aber die Rede von jenen Greueln, von denen man kurz nach 1945 ohnehin erwartet hatte, daß sie zur Sprache kommen würden, kann durchaus den einen oder anderen Skandal hervorrufen.[7]

Die Figur Speers ist übrigens ein Schlüssel zu dieser Verkehrung. Für Auschwitz nahm er in Nürnberg die Mitverantwortung, später die Mitschuld auf sich – bei gleichzeitiger Leugnung, jemals etwas Genaues gewußt zu haben. Er hätte, so gab er zu, wissen müssen, und dies mache ihn zum Mitschuldigen. Hiermit hatte Speer eine nahezu geniale Formel gefunden. Es war das – von ihm wie von der deutschen Bevölkerung – verlangte Bekenntnis zur Mitverantwortung, es war mehr, ein Schuldbekenntnis – ganz individuell, aber jeder konnte einstimmen – zudem auf so hohem Niveau, daß es ihn beinahe adelte. Eine, wie gesagt, nahezu geniale Formel, man kann – angesichts der bewußten und nachweisbaren Lügen über das Ausmaß dessen, was er tatsächlich nicht nur gewußt, sondern gesehen hatte – sagen, eine Formel von ebenso atemberaubender Dreistigkeit[8] wie durchschlagendem Erfolg.

Hatte die Spaltung des Holocaust in zwei säuberlich voneinander geschiedene Vorgänge – das Töten in den Vernichtungslagern durch eine mörderische Elite und das Töten als scheinbar kriegsförmiger Akt, durch unterschiedlich uniformierte Einheiten exekutiert – dazu geführt, zunächst die historische Einmaligkeit der Vernichtungslager zu übersehen, dann nur noch diese in den Blick zu nehmen, so ist das Resultat ein bis heute nicht zureichendes Verständnis der Gewaltdynamik selbst. Denn für beide Teile gilt: „Der Holocaust hat sich letzten Endes deshalb ereignet, weil auf einfachster Ebene gesehen einzelne Menschen über einen längeren Zeitraum hinweg andere Menschen zu Abertausenden umgebracht haben."[9] Das systematische Unterbewerten des Antisemitismus ist von diesem Umstand nicht zu trennen.

7 Vgl. auch Sereny, a.a.O., S.401f.

8 Vgl. dazu vor allem Sereny, a.a.O., S.678f, 654f.

9 Christopher Browning, Ganz normale Männer. Das Reserve-Polizeibataillon 101 und die „Endlösung" in Polen, Reinbek 1996, S.13.

When people accuse Daniel Goldhagen of falling into modes of explanation that date back to the 50s, they are wrongly insinuating that he grasps anti-Semitism in categories of propaganda and indoctrination, regards it as the decisive factor in an escalating dynamic. In Goldhagen's book, however, anti-Semitism appears as a communication system, a code with which a majority of Germans very quickly could come to an agreement about what was true and false. It was precisely the wide dissemination and implicit use of this code that often kept anti-Semitism below the threshold of perception. Telford Taylor reports in retrospect how the judges at Nuremberg would not have paid any notice to Dönitz's statement that naturally he was of the opinion that a necessary prerequisite for Germany's military power had been the exclusion of the Jewish element from the German national community, because Dönitz, who of course claimed he had never been an anti-Semite, had himself not noticed that his judges would see anything out of the ordinary in such a statement.[10] The trial of Police Battalion 101, which is investigated by both Christopher Browning and Daniel Goldhagen, proves that in the 60s and 70s[11] the question of an anti-Semitic consensus was no longer posed, which is why the topic no longer appears in the court records or, as a result, in Browning's book. Once the court had excluded the topic, the murderers could provide only fragmentary information about their deed: "A few of the policemen made the attempt to confront the question of choice, but failed to find the words. It was a different time and place, as if they had been on another political planet, and the political values and vocabulary of the 1960s were useless in explaining the situation in which they had found themselves in 1942."[12] As Goldhagen shows, it was only by indirectly speaking of an anti-Semitic phantasm that, prior to their first killing mission, the troop could come to an understanding of its necessity.[13]

10 Telford Taylor, The Anatomy of the Nuremberg Trials (New York: 1992), p. 406.

11 The investigations ran from 1962–87.

12 Browning, op. cit., p. 72.

13 Cf. Goldhagen, op. cit., p. 212.

Wenn man Daniel Goldhagen vorwirft, er falle in Erklärungsmuster der 50er Jahre zurück, unterstellt man ihm fälschlicherweise, er fasse den Antisemitismus als entscheidenden Faktor in einer Eskalationsdynamik in Kategorien von Propaganda und Indoktrination. Bei Goldhagen erscheint aber der Antisemitismus als ein Verständigungssystem, ein Code, mit dem sich eine Majorität der Deutschen sehr schnell über richtig und falsch verständigen kann. Es war gerade die weite Verbreitung und selbstverständliche Verwendung dieses Codes, die ihn oft unterhalb der Wahrnehmungsschwelle hielt. Telford Taylor berichtet rückblickend, wie die Richter von Nürnberg Dönitz' Satz, er sei selbstverständlich der Meinung gewesen, die Ausschaltung der Juden aus der deutschen Volksgemeinschaft sei die unabdingbare Voraussetzung für Deutschlands militärische Stärke gewesen, darum nicht bemerkt hätten, weil Dönitz, der von sich natürlich behauptete, niemals Antisemit gewesen zu sein, selber nicht bemerkt habe, daß seinen Richtern an dieser Aussage etwas hätte auffallen können.[10] – Der Prozeß gegen das von Christopher Browning wie von Daniel Goldhagen untersuchte Polizeibataillon 101 zeigt, daß in den 60er und 70er Jahren[11] die Frage nach einem antisemitischen Konsens nicht mehr gestellt wurde, weshalb dieses Thema in den Gerichtsakten nicht mehr und in Folge dessen bei Browning nicht vorkommt. Nachdem das Gericht dieses Thema ausschließt, können die Mörder über ihre Tat nur noch fragmentarische Auskunft geben: „Ein paar der Täter machten den Versuch, sich der Frage nach der eigenen Entscheidungsfreiheit zu stellen, fanden aber nicht die entsprechenden Worte – so als wären sie früher politisch auf einem fernen Planeten gewesen und nun an einen anderen Ort und in eine ganz andere Zeit – die der sechziger Jahre – verschlagen worden, deren politische Wertvorstellungen und dessen Vokabular sich nicht zur Erklärung jener Lage gebrauchen ließen, in der sie sich 1942 befunden hatten."[12] Nur indirekt läßt sich, wie Goldhagen zeigt, nachweisen, wie sich die Truppe über ein antisemitisches Phantasma vor dem ersten Mordeinsatz über dessen Notwendigkeit verständigt.[13]

10 Telford Taylor, Die Nürnberger Prozesse. Hintergründe, Analysen und Erkenntnisse aus heutiger Sicht, München 1994, S.472.

11 Die Ermittlungen laufen von 1962-87.

12 Browning, a.a.O., S.106.

13 Vgl. etwa Goldhagen, a.a.O., S.295ff.

The loss of the vocabulary in which one can speak about motives and preferences of action brings with it the loss of any notion of free choice, which, as the records prove beyond a doubt, had been present: "Most of the interrogated police denied they had any choice."[14] The words with which they could have described why they acted as the had, why they had felt what they had done was right, were no longer available to them. The court had no interest in their being uttered again, and the defendants surely knew that their use would have been anything but helpful to them. And here the viewpoint one ought to take of such matters in a court of law can be instructive for historiography: a confession that one has taken part in the killing of Jews because one considered Jews inferior and dangerous, should not have led to acquittal on the grounds of unaccountability due to indoctrination and propaganda, but to a conviction based on admitted base motives.

It would be incorrect if I were to advance Daniel Goldhagen's book merely as an indication that things have changed somewhat in our country. A book is not only accepted, but it also serves to make people aware of, and to help them reformulate, their readiness to accept those things with which it deals, for mere diffuse sentiment does not suffice. I believe that with this Democracy Prize, the Journal for German and International Politics wanted to express their gratitude that with his book – and this can surely be said even at such close temporal proximity – he has made a contribution to the discussion of historical factual material, a contribution that can never be ignored in the future and that – and I say this in the face of those political sectors who currently are busy loudly protesting that there has been any progress whatever in this direction – alone is in a position to overcome what Hannah Arendt, on a visit to Germany in 1950, saw as a "general lack of emotion," "an apparent heartlessness, sometimes covered over with cheap sentimentality," that is "only the most conspicuous outward symptom of a deep-rooted, stubborn, and at times vicious refusal to face and come to terms with what really happened."[15]

Translation by John E. Woods

14 Browning, op. cit., p. 72.

15 Hannah Arendt, "The Aftermath of Nazi Rule: Report from Germany," in: Essays in Understanding 1930–1954 (New York: 1994), p. 249.

Mit dem Wegfall des Vokabulars, in dem über Gründe und Handlungspräferenzen gesprochen werden kann, fällt auch die Vorstellung einer freien Entscheidung, die, wie die Akten zweifelsfrei belegen, gegeben gewesen ist, weg: „Die meisten der vernommenen Polizisten bestritten, überhaupt eine Wahl gehabt zu haben.“[14] Die Wörter, mit denen sie hätten beschreiben können, warum sie gehandelt hatten, wie sie gehandelt hatten, warum sie für richtig gehalten hatten, was sie getan hatten, standen nicht mehr zur Verfügung. Das Gericht hatte kein Interesse daran, sie wieder zur Sprache zu bringen, und die Angeklagten dürften gewußt haben, daß ihnen ihre Verwendung alles andere als nützlich gewesen wäre. Hier mag die vor Gericht einzunehmende Sicht der Dinge, die Historiographie belehren: ein Bekenntnis dazu, man habe sich darum an den Judenmorden beteiligt, weil man die Juden für minderwertig und gefährlich gehalten habe, hätte ja nicht zu einem Freispruch wegen Zurechnungsunfähigkeit auf Grund von Indoktrination und Propaganda, sondern zu einer Verurteilung bei Zuerkennung niederer Beweggründe geführt.

Es wäre ungerecht, wenn ich Daniel Goldhagens Buch nur als Indikator dafür anführen würde, daß sich etwas geändert hat hierzulande. Ein Buch wird ja nicht nur angenommen, sondern es dient zur Bewußtmachung und zur Neuformulierung der Bereitschaft, das, wovon es handelt, zu akzeptieren, denn das bloß diffuse Gefühl reicht ja nicht aus. Ich denke, daß die „Blätter für deutsche und internationale Politik“ mit ihrem Demokratiepreis ihren Dank dafür aussprechen wollten, daß er mit seinem Buch einen – das läßt sich wohl auch aus der großen zeitlichen Nähe heraus sagen – nicht mehr wegzudenkenden Beitrag zu jener Diskussion des historischen Faktenmaterials leistet, die allein – und ich sage das angesichts jener politischen Sektoren, die gegenwärtig dabei sind, jeden Fortschritt in dieser Diskussion lauthals zu dementieren – in der Lage ist, den von Hannah Arendt bei ihrem Deutschlandbesuch 1950 konstatierten „allgemeine(n) Gefühlsmangel“ und jene „offensichtliche Herzlosigkeit, die manchmal mit billiger Rührseligkeit kaschiert wird“, zu überwinden, „die nur das auffälligste äußerliche Symptom einer tief verwurzelten, hartnäckigen und gelegentlich brutalen Weigerung“ seien, „sich dem tatsächlich Geschehenen zu stellen und sich damit abzufinden.“[15]

14 Browning, a.a.O.

15 Hannah Arendt, Besuch in Deutschland, in: dies., Zur Zeit. Politische Essays, Berlin 1986, S.44.

Daniel Jonah Goldhagen

Modell Bundesrepublik

National History, Democracy, and Internationalization in Germany

George Santayana's famous aphorism, "those who cannot remember the past are condemned to repeat it", captures something important about the relationship between learning from the past and political action. Yet it is contestable. What he might have said – though it would have been less lapidary, and therefore perhaps none of us would now know it – is "those who study history, may learn from it, and may therefore be less likely to repeat its darkest chapters." If I understand the Blätter correctly, then it is this non-aphoristic formulation that informs its members' thinking.

I share this view and wish to use this occasion to discuss facets of the learning of history and of democracy in the Federal Republic, and to suggest that the success of each are related.

How does one learn from history? How does a nation learn from history? Whatever else is necessary, an accurate and properly interpreted history has to be available. This requires that certain proclivities in the writing of history, and here I speak specifically of national history, must be resisted, or more likely, counteracted.

By national history I do not mean here just the history of a given country or nation. I refer to the dominant framework for understanding that history. This is not confined to or necessarily governed by how academic history is written, though it may include that. It encompasses how a national history is represented more generally in the public sphere – in newspapers and magazines, in television and film, in school

Daniel Jonah Goldhagen

Modell Bundesrepublik

Nationalgeschichte, Demokratie und Internationalisierung in Deutschland

„Wer sich der Vergangenheit nicht erinnern kann, ist verdammt, sie zu wiederholen." Dieser berühmte Aphorismus von George Santayana erfaßt einen wichtigen Punkt im Verhältnis zwischen Lernen aus der Geschichte und politischem Handeln. Er ist jedoch anfechtbar. Obgleich weniger prägnant und daher wohl keinem von uns heute mehr geläufig, hätte er anders formuliert werden können – etwa folgendermaßen: „Wer sich mit der Geschichte befaßt, kann aus ihr lernen und ist somit vermutlich weniger anfällig, deren dunkle Kapitel zu wiederholen." Wie ich die „Blätter" verstehe, orientiert die Zeitschrift sich an dieser nicht-aphoristischen Variante des Gedankens.

Ich teile diese Auffassung, und ich möchte diese Gelegenheit zum Anlaß nehmen, bestimmte Facetten des Lernens aus der Geschichte und der Demokratie in der Bundesrepublik zu erörtern. Auf diese Art läßt sich zeigen, daß der Erfolg des einen mit dem des anderen zusammenhängt.

Wie lernt man aus der Geschichte? Wie lernt eine Nation aus der Geschichte? Was immer ansonsten notwendig sein mag – es muß eine zuverlässig dokumentierte und zutreffend interpretierte Geschichte geben. Vor allem bezogen auf die Nationalgeschichte setzt das voraus, daß Geschichtsschreibung bestimmten Versuchungen widersteht, besser noch: ihnen entgegenwirkt.

Mit Nationalgeschichte meine ich nicht allein die Geschichte eines bestimmten Landes oder einer bestimmten Nation. Ich spreche von dem Rahmen, der das Geschichtsverständnis bestimmt. Diesen Rahmen prägt nicht unbedingt die akademische Geschichtsschreibung, obwohl sie dazu beitragen kann. Der Rahmen schließt ein, wie Nationalgeschichte in der breiteren Öffentlichkeit dargestellt wird – in Zeitungen und Zeitschriften, im Fernsehen

textbooks and popular works of history, and in public memorials and rituals. These shape a people's images of its past far more than do the scholarly books of academic historians.

Because national histories are principally composed by members of the nation, they bear some obvious relationship to autobiographies. The author and the subject of autobiography are the same. The authors and the subjects of national history share an identity. Autobiographies generally present their subjects in an overly favorable light. National histories generally prettify and glorify their subject, the nation's past. Autobiography tends towards individual narcissistic self-exaltation, namely self-hagiography. National history tends towards collective narcissistic self-exaltation, namely nationalist history.

Developing an accurate view of each requires that the subjects be cast in the critical light of outside perspectives. For the portrait of the individual, the outside perspective comes from the biographer. For national history, the external perspective comes from abroad. But, because composing national history differs from providing an account of one person's life, merely having available an external perspective is not enough.

The individual's portrait – whatever the success of an autobiography – does not remain in that individual's hands. For national history, it is the opposite. Because – whatever the success of external perspectives – national history does not pass into the hands of those outside the nation but continues to be composed by members of the nation, by those who share the identity of their subjects. It continues to be composed in a country's own newspapers, television, textbooks, and history books.

So, unlike the rendering of an individual's life, the writing of an accurate national history requires that some outside perspectives be integrally incorporated into the composition of national history itself, which means into the framework of understanding used by the people who must depict subjects with whom they share a fundamental identi-

und im Kino, in Schulbüchern, populärwissenschaftlichen Darstellungen, bei Gedenkveranstaltungen und Ritualen. Das alles formt die Vorstellungen eines Volkes von seiner Geschichte viel nachhaltiger als gelehrte Werke.

Da Nationalgeschichte hauptsächlich von Angehörigen der betreffenden Nation entworfen wird, hat sie zumeist etwas autobiographisches. Bei einer Autobiographie sind Autor und Gegenstand identisch. Auch bei einer Nationalgeschichte teilen Autoren und Gegenstand eine Identität. Autobiographien rücken ihren Gegenstand meist in ein übertrieben vorteilhaftes Licht. Auch Nationalgeschichten beschönigen und verherrlichen normalerweise ihre Inhalte, die Vergangenheit einer Nation. Autobiographien neigen zu narzistischer Selbstüberhöhung, das heißt Legendenbildung. Ebenso neigen Nationalgeschichten zu kollektiver, narzistischer Verzückung, zur nationalistischen Geschichtsschreibung.

Ein genaues Verständnis erfordert in beiden Fällen eines: die jeweiligen Gegenstände in das Licht einer kritischen Außenwahrnehmung zu rücken. Bei den Persönlichkeitsportraits fällt das in die Zuständigkeit des Biographen. Im Falle der Nationalgeschichte besorgt es das Ausland. Nun unterscheiden sich Berichte über die Vitae Einzelner vom Entwurf einer Nationalgeschichte. Und deshalb reichen, in bezug auf die Nationalgeschichte, Außenbilder nicht aus.

Wie erfolgreich auch immer die Autobiographie sein mag – das Portrait des Einzelnen bleibt nicht in dessen Hand. Bei der Geschichte einer Nation verhält es sich genau umgekehrt. Ganz gleich, welchen Einfluß die Sichtweisen Außenstehender gewinnen – eine Nationalgeschichte geht nicht in die Hände jener über, die nicht dieser Nation angehören. Nationalgeschichte wird von Angehörigen eben dieser Nation entworfen, also Menschen, die mit jenen, über die sie schreiben, die Identität teilen. Einheimische Zeitungen, das Fernsehen, Lehr- und Geschichtsbücher tragen ihren Teil bei.

Eine zutreffende Nationalgeschichte erfordert daher, anders als die Beschreibung einer individuellen Lebensgeschichte, die Einbeziehung und Verarbeitung der Sichtweisen Außenstehender. Diese externen Sichtweisen sollten einfließen in den Interpretationsrahmen derer, die es sich zur Aufgabe gemacht haben, Subjekte darzustellen, mit denen sie ei-

ty. This is rare. Yet, as I shall discuss in a moment, it has happened, to some great extent, in the Federal Republic of Germany.

Turning to politics, I need hardly belabor the point that the nation state tends towards nationalism, the exercise of power and the pursuit of its own material, positional, and symbolic interests to the detriment of other states and other peoples. Democracy serves to counteract these tendencies (though without guaranteed success, witness the history of colonialism). Democracies go to war, particularly against each other, with far less frequency than non-democracies do – indeed it has almost never happened. Democracies have far more cooperative and mutually beneficial economic relations. The balance between emphasizing the welfare of their own citizens, on the one hand, and pursuing international power or prestige, on the other, is more heavily weighted to domestic well-being among democracies than among non-democracies.

Yet democratic institutions alone fetter the nationalist tendencies of elites (and of peoples) imperfectly, particularly when a country is far more powerful then its neighbors. This has been recognized as a problem throughout the history of the Federal Republic. Yet these nationalist aspirations have, by and large, been tempered or certainly, held in check, to an extent that few would have imagined in 1945 or 1949.

Two parallel, indeed surprising, developments characterize the Federal Republic: the emergence of a relatively non-nationalist and remarkably self-critical, national history and a relatively non-nationalist, internationally responsible nation state.

In my view, these developments are not unrelated. A powerful, common mechanism has influenced the development both of historical understanding and of democracy in the Federal Republic: internationalization.

Historical understanding and democracy in the Federal Republic are related in another way. The development of an appropriate general framework for understanding the past has been critical in the development of a responsible democratic political system.

ne grundlegende Identität teilen. Das geschieht selten – in der Bundesrepublik jedoch in hohem Maße.

Was die Politik angeht, bedarf es keiner weiteren Erläuterung, daß der Nationalstaat zu Nationalismus und zu Machtpolitik neigt und bemüht ist, die eigenen Interessen zu Lasten anderer Länder und Völker durchzusetzen. Die Demokratie hilft, solchen Tendenzen entgegenzuwirken – ohne Erfolgsgarantie, wie die Geschichte des Kolonialismus zeigt. Demokratien führen seltener Kriege, besonders gegeneinander, als Nicht-Demokratien. Tatsächlich gab es kaum je Kriege zwischen Demokratien. Ihre Wirtschaftsbeziehungen sind in der Regel kooperativer und für beide Seiten gewinnbringend. Demokratien wägen ab, ob sie das Wohl der eigenen Bürger in den Vordergrund rücken, oder ob sie nach internationaler Macht streben wollen. Im Ergebnis messen sie der Wohlfahrt mehr Bedeutung bei als Nicht-Demokratien.

Demokratischen Institutionen gelingt es allerdings nur unzureichend, nationalistische Tendenzen der Eliten und der Völker in den Griff zu bekommen. Das gilt vor allem dann, wenn ein Land viel mächtiger ist als seine Nachbarn. In der ganzen Geschichte der Bundesrepublik war dies als Problem präsent. Das Ergebnis: Nationalistische Bestrebungen wurden im großen und ganzen gemäßigt oder in Schach gehalten. Und dies in einem Maße, wie es sich 1945 oder vier Jahre später bei Gründung der Bundesrepublik nur wenige hätten vorstellen können.

Zwei parallel verlaufende, überraschende Entwicklungen kennzeichnen die Bundesrepublik: Das eine ist die Herausbildung einer relativ nicht-nationalistischen und bemerkenswert selbstkritischen Nationalgeschichte, das andere die Entstehung eines relativ wenig nationalistischen, international verantwortungsvoll agierenden Nationalstaates.

Meiner Meinung nach gibt es da einen Zusammenhang. Der gleiche mächtige Mechanismus hat die Entwicklung sowohl des historischen Selbstverständnisses als auch der Demokratie in der Bundesrepublik beeinflußt: ihre Internationalisierung.

Geschichtsverständnis und Demokratie hängen in der Bundesrepublik aber auch in anderer Hinsicht zusammen. Die Entwicklung eines angemessenen Rahmens für die Sicht der Vergangenheit hat wesentlich zum Entstehen eines politischen Systems verantwortungsbewußter Demokratie beigetragen.

I began thinking about these issues when, at an academic conference last fall, the discussant on a panel mentioned that German history had been "internationalized." Unlike the history of other major countries (and probably most countries), the main contours of modern German history have not been drawn solely by Germans. The commentator observed that more professors of German history teach at American universities than at German universities. No matter how Germans would like to write their own history, a powerful external check exists from abroad.

However some in Germany might have wished or even tried to write a sanitized German history, it has simply not been possible because it would have necessitated altering the dominant framework of understanding, which has not been entirely under national control. Whatever the challenges to it or variations upon it, this framework consists of these only sometimes arti-culated notions:

1. Nazism was not an accident of German history.

2. The rise of Nazism is owed fundamentally to the failure to develop in Germany a genuine understanding and sufficient acceptance of democratic beliefs and liberal values and therefore to produce sustainable democratic institutions.

3. The Holocaust was not accidental to, but an organic outgrowth of, Nazism.

4. The Holocaust was therefore made possible by the failure to develop a firm national democratic orientation and political system.

5. Because the unsurpassed catastrophe that was the Holocaust was not an accident, it (even more than Nazism itself) is the central event of modern German history. Because the failure to develop a democratic orientation and a sustainable political system made the Holocaust possible, this failure is its central feature.

Now it may be that, had a defeated Germany in 1945 been left to rebuild itself in accordance with its own purely domestic political impulses, then this

Über diese Dinge begann ich im vergangenen Herbst nachzudenken. Auf einer wissenschaftlichen Konferenz hatte ein Diskussionsteilnehmer bemerkt, die deutsche Geschichte sei „internationalisiert" worden. Anders als in anderen gewichtigen (und anders als vermutlich in den meisten Ländern), wurden die Konturen der modernen deutschen Nationalgeschichte nicht ausschließlich von Deutschen gezeichnet. Der Redner wies darauf hin, daß mehr Professoren für deutsche Geschichte an amerikanischen Universitäten lehren als an deutschen. Ganz gleich, wie die Deutschen ihre eigene Geschichte am liebsten schreiben würden – was sie tun, wird im Ausland sehr aufmerksam verfolgt.

Sicher mag mancher in Deutschland den Wunsch gehegt und versucht haben, eine bereinigte Version der deutschen Geschichte zu schreiben. Durchsetzen konnten sich solche Ambitionen nicht. Dazu hätte man den gegebenen, nicht komplett unter nationaler Kontrolle stehenden Deutungsrahmen ersetzen müssen. Was immer dessen Varianten und Alternativen sind, er beinhaltet die folgenden, nur gelegentlich ausgesprochenen Grundthesen:

1. Der Nazismus war kein Betriebsunfall der deutschen Geschichte.

2. Der Aufstieg des Nazismus beruhte im wesentlichen darauf, daß es in Deutschland nicht gelang, genuines Verständnis und eine ausreichende Akzeptanz für demokratische Überzeugungen sowie liberale Werte zu entwickeln und es deshalb ebenfalls nicht gelang, demokratische Institutionen nachhaltig zu etablieren.

3. Der Holocaust war kein Zufall nazistischer Herrschaft, sondern ein organisches Resultat derselben.

4. Der Holocaust konnte also geschehen, weil eine beständige demokratische Orientierung und ein ebensolches politisches System in Deutschland nicht zustande gekommen waren.

5. Weil der Holocaust, diese beispiellose Katastrophe, kein Zufall war, ist er mehr noch als der Nazismus selbst – das zentrale Ereignis der modernen deutschen Geschichte.Und weil das Fehlen einer soliden demokratischen Orientierung und eines entsprechenden politischen Systems den Holocaust erst möglich machte, ist dieses doppelte Scheitern ihr zentrales Charakteristikum.

Mag sein, daß sich jener Interpretationsrahmen auch dann entwickelt und durchgesetzt hätte, wäre das besiegte Deutschland 1945 beim politi-

framework of understanding would still have developed and become dominant within Germany. I doubt it. But it did develop and it did so, in part, because the understanding of German national history both in the Federal Republic's popular media and also in the academy was subject to international influence. The consequences of this internationalization of German historical composition are significant.

In the Federal Republic, people have been exposed to a more accurate account of their own history than they otherwise would be and than the peoples of other countries typically are. There is no other country of which I know that has dealt so openly and consistently with the inglorious and horrific portions of its own past as has the Federal Republic. This does not mean that the record in Germany has been perfect. Far from it. But in comparative terms, the public discourse about German history looks extraordinarily honest.

External pressure has, to some extent, induced Germans to do this. Because so much attention outside of the Federal Republic has been paid to German history, specifically to the Holocaust, and to how Germans discuss, commemorate, and deal with their past, Germans' treatment of their own history has been an international political issue and has been seen at times, rightly or wrongly, as an indicator of Germans' political rectitude, specifically that they have rejected and abandoned all that was Nazism.

Internationalization has taken a second form: the direct involvement by non-Germans in the composition of German national history; on television, for example, with the *Holocaust* series; in film, by among many other examples, *Schindler's List*; and in the academy by an array of non-German authors who have written books considered to be standard works. But the dominant framework for understanding German national history did not develop as it has merely because it was imposed from outside or because non-Germans have had access to the institutions of the German public sphere.

A third aspect of the internationalization of national history writing has been the enormous influence of these outside perspectives upon the perspectives of those in Germany who have shaped the understanding of national history and who continue the ongoing process of framing

schen Wiederaufbau sich selbst überlassen geblieben. Ich bezweifele das. Jedenfalls hat er sich entwickelt. Und das auch deshalb, weil das Verständnis deutscher Nationalgeschichte in den Medien wie im akademischen Bereich der Bundesrepublik internationalen Einflüssen unterlag. Diese Internationalisierung der deutschen Geschichtsschreibung hat weitreichende Folgen.

In der Bundesrepublik sind die Menschen mit einer genaueren Darstellung ihrer Geschichte konfrontiert, als Bürger anderer Länder es gewöhnt sind. Ich kenne kein anderes Land, das so offen und konsequent mit den unrühmlichen und schrecklichen Kapiteln der eigenen Vergangenheit umgeht. Das heißt nicht, Deutschland zu verklären. Ganz und gar nicht. Aber im internationalen Vergleich erscheint der öffentliche Diskurs über die deutsche Geschichte bemerkenswert ehrlich.

Der Druck von außen hat dazu beigetragen. Der Umgang der Deutschen mit ihrer Geschichte ist zu einem Thema der internationalen Politik geworden – in erster Linie natürlich der Holocaust. Die Einstellung zur eigenen Geschichte galt zeitweise, ob zu Recht oder zu Unrecht, als Maßstab politischer Vertrauenswürdigkeit – vor allem hinsichtlich der Frage, ob die Deutschen der Bundesrepublik alles Nazistische aufgegeben haben.

Die Internationalisierung hat einen zweiten Aspekt: die unmittelbare Beteiligung Nichtdeutscher an der Gestaltung der deutschen Nationalgeschichte – im Fernsehen mit der Holocaust-Serie, im Kino mit „Schindlers Liste“ und vielen anderen Filmen, im akademischen Bereich mit einer stattlichen Zahl nichtdeutscher Autoren, deren Bücher als Standardwerke gelten. Um Mißverständnissen vorzubeugen: Der existierende Interpretationsrahmen in Sachen deutscher Geschichte wurde nicht einfach von außen auferlegt. Und er entwickelte sich nicht allein deshalb, weil Nichtdeutsche Zugang zur deutschen Öffentlichkeit besaßen.

Ein dritter Aspekt der Internationalisierung ist der starke Einfluß von außen kommender Sichtweisen auf jene Deutsche, die das Verständnis der Nationalgeschichte geformt haben und die den ständigen Prozeß der Erfassung und Auslegung der Vergangenheit vorantreiben. Der Einfluß stand in

and interpreting the past. This influence did dovetail with these Germans' own democratic beliefs and values, which, if at first haltingly, gradually became dominant in the Federal Republic. The democratic aspirations of the first postwar generation of Germans, the "sixty-eighters", produced independent demands for a more accurate reckoning with the past.

These three aspects of the internationalization of German national history writing – pressure from the outside, direct participation by outsiders, and the intellectual influence of external perspectives – have, at their core, a common feature: the incorporation of the critical perspectives of outsiders into national history, in what might be called a pluralized national history (or at least a more pluralized national history). It is not a coincidence that the country that has succeeded best at dealing honestly with the least savory part of its past, Germany, is the country that has had the least control over the construction of its national history. There is a more positive way to frame this. Germans have succeeded best at constructing an accurate national history because, drawing on both domestic and international sources, they have succeeded best at counteracting the prettifying, mythologizing, and self-deluding tendencies of national history writing.

II

With German democracy, similar features can be observed. The development of a democratic orientation among the vast majority of Germans and of stable democratic institutions in the Federal Republic is the great cultural and political success story of the postwar period. The transformation from Nazi Germany to a genuinely democratic Federal Republic did not, of course, occur overnight. It too had much to do with the internationalization of German political life, which continues to this day.

This internationalization has had three dimensions analogous to the three that have influenced national history writing. The western part of Germany was initially given no choice but to adopt democratic institutions.

Einklang mit deren eigenen demokratischen Überzeugungen und Wertvorstellungen, die sich in der Bundesrepublik zunächst stockend, dann immer nachhaltiger durchsetzten. Die demokratischen Bestrebungen der ersten Nachkriegsgeneration, der Achtundsechziger, brachten dann eigenständige Forderungen nach einem angemessenen Umgang mit der Vergangenheit hervor.

Druck von außen, direkte Beteiligung Außenstehender, der intellektuelle Einfluß nichtdeutscher Sichtweisen – diese drei Aspekte der Internationalisierung deutscher Nationalgeschichtsschreibung haben im Kern ein gemeinsames Merkmal: die Integration kritischer Perspektiven Außenstehender in das Verständnis der deutschen Nationalgeschichte. Das Ergebnis läßt sich als pluralisierte Nationalgeschichte – oder zumindest stärker pluralisierte Nationalgeschichte – bezeichnen. Es ist kein Zufall, daß das Land, dem es am besten gelungen ist, ehrlich mit den weniger angenehmen Kapiteln seiner Vergangenheit umzugehen, zugleich das Land ist, das die geringste Kontrolle über die Konstruktion seiner Nationalgeschichte gehabt hat. Positiver formuliert: Den Deutschen ist es am besten gelungen, eine wahrheitsgemäße Nationalgeschichte zu schreiben, weil durch die Einbeziehung nationaler wie internationaler Quellen den beschönigenden, mythologisierenden und selbsttäuschenden Tendenzen nationaler Geschichtsschreibung erfolgreich entgegengewirkt wurde.

II

Ähnliches kann man für die Demokratie in Deutschland feststellen. Die demokratische Orientierung der großen Mehrheit und stabile demokratische Institutionen – diese beiden Entwicklungen stehen für die große kulturelle und politische Erfolgsgeschichte der Nachkriegszeit überhaupt. Der Übergang von Nazi-Deutschland in eine demokratische Bundesrepublik fand natürlich nicht über Nacht statt. Auch diese Transformation hat viel mit der anhaltenden Internationalisierung des deutschen politischen Lebens zu tun.

Diese Internationalisierung hat, analog zu jener in puncto Geschichtsschreibung, ebenfalls drei Dimensionen. Dem Westteil Deutschlands blieb anfangs keine andere Wahl, als die demokratischen Institutionen zu über-

(Many adopted them gladly not only because they believed in democracy's desirability but also because the threat from the communist east during the 1950s made the western camp the only feasible choice.) Second, German sovereignty has also been penetrated, and therefore circumscribed, by the absence of full sovereignty until 1955, then by the continuing presence of mainly American troops as part of NATO, and also by the growth of the European Union. Finally, the development of the Federal Republic's political self-understanding has emerged at least partly through the internalization of the values of their conquerors who then became their allies. In these and other ways, the conduct of the Federal Republic has, over the years, been greatly influenced by the views of others.

This internationalization of the Federal Republic can be seen in two characteristics of its elites. No other major country has an elite that is so internationalized and comfortable in a second language. Not the US, France, Italy, Britain, Russia, China, or Japan. (This linguistic facility is undoubtedly also true of the German people compared to their counterparts in other major countries.) The political elites of no other major country seem to have cared as much about how they are viewed abroad as have those of the Federal Republic. Aside from matters that directly and tangibly affect their interests, the American, British, and French political elites care little for how their actions are viewed abroad. In Germany, this "other-directedness" has led to the incorporation of outside perspectives into the decision-making of German politics more than it has in other countries.

Looking at oneself through the eyes of others is a self-correcting mechanism. In the case of Germany, such a gaze revealed its neighbors frequent suspicion and apprehension at what a rebuilt, then resurgent, then united, and powerful or even dominant Germany might do. This, among other things, has contributed to turning Germany – with all the disheartening exceptions – into a responsible actor in international affairs, especially in the evolution of the European Union, though also beyond.

Without minimizing the powerful domestic sources for the enormous accomplishments of German democracy, democracy's success

nehmen. (Viele übernahmen sie gern – nicht nur weil sie die Demokratie für etwas Wünschenswertes hielten; die Bedrohung durch den kommunistischen Osten machte das westliche Lager zur einzig attraktiven Wahl.) Zweitens, die Bundesrepublik wurde durch das Fehlen voller Souveränität bis 1955, danach von der Präsenz vor allem amerikanischer Truppen sowie von der Konkretisierung der europäischen Integration eingehegt und geprägt. Schließlich gingen wichtige Impulse für das entstehende bundesrepublikanische Selbstverständnis von der Verinnerlichung der Wertvorstellungen der Siegermächte aus, die später zu Verbündeten wurden. Auf diese Weise prägte der Einfluß anderer über Jahre hinweg das Verhalten der Bundesrepublik.

Diese Internationalisierung der Bundesrepublik läßt sich anhand zweier Merkmale nachzeichnen: Kein anderes bedeutendes Land besitzt eine Elite, die so international orientiert ist und die sich derart in einer oder mehreren Fremdsprachen zu Hause fühlt – weder die USA, noch Frankreich, Italien, Großbritannien, Rußland, China oder Japan. (Diese relativ größere Sprachkompetenz gilt übrigens auch für die Deutschen insgesamt.) In keinem anderen bedeutenden Land scheint sich die politische Elite so viel daraus zu machen, wie man im Ausland über sie denkt. Abgesehen von Angelegenheiten, die ihre Interessen direkt berühren, ist es den amerikanischen, britischen und französischen Eliten einigermaßen gleichgültig, wie das Ausland ihr Handeln bewertet. Diese Art von „Fremdbestimmung" hat in der Bundesrepublik dazu geführt, daß die Sichtweisen Außenstehender mehr als anderswo in die Entscheidungsprozesse der Politik einbezogen werden.

Sich mit den Augen anderer zu betrachten, ist ein Mechanismus der Selbstkorrektur. Im Fall Deutschland offenbart dieser Blick Besorgnis und Mißtrauen der Nachbarn hinsichtlich dessen, was ein wiederaufgebautes und wieder erstarkendes, später wiedervereinigtes, mächtiges, ja sogar dominantes Deutschland anrichten könnte. Das hat mit dazubeigetragen, daß die Bundesrepublik – trotz aller Ausnahmen – zu einem verantwortungsbewußten internationalen Akteur wurde, vor allem, was die Europäische Union anbelangt.

Ich will den bemerkenswerten Beitrag einheimischer Kräfte zu den Erfolgen der deutschen Demokratie nicht abwerten. Aber: Der Erfolg der Demo-

at home and the Federal Republic's comparatively good record as a member of the community of nations is significantly owing to its internationalization.

German national history and German democracy are connected by more than their common internationalization. Knowledge of history has itself been critical for the success of the Federal Republic.

I mentioned earlier that for people to learn from their history, they must have an accurate account of it. The internationalization of German history has helped to that end. Still, what sorts of learning take place and how has the Federal Republic, in particular, benefited from such learning? Two kinds strike me as particularly relevant.

The first is the learning from the past that is self-consciously and explicitly undertaken in order to provide a (how-to) guide to constructing a different future. A classic, successful example can be seen in the construction of the Federal Republic's political system. Its framers crafted many of its crucial features in order to make the re-emergence of Nazism less likely, which included avoiding the institutional weaknesses of the Weimar political system.

A second kind of learning is not so self-conscious and goal-directed. It is people's reassessment of their beliefs and values in light of experience and in light of competing beliefs and values. This takes place every day, by every person. Sometimes, the vast majority of the people of a given society learn from common experience in the same way. This happens typically after a national trauma, or when fundamental institutions of society are transformed. Examples besides Germany include Japan, which after World War II transformed its deeply militaristic culture into one that now has a strong pacifist component, and the whites of the American South, who with the overthrow of legal segregation have substantially altered their understanding of the place of blacks in society.

This learning process is not automatic or overnight. It is gradual. In the case of the Federal Republic the important learning occurred principally during the first two postwar decades, and here I refer to democra-

kratie und das vergleichsweise gute Abschneiden der Bundesrepublik als Mitglied der Staatengemeinschaft sind in bedeutendem Maße auf die Internationalisierung zurückzuführen.

Deutsche Nationalgeschichte und deutsche Demokratie sind durch mehr als die beiden gemeinsame Internationalisierung miteinander verbunden. Das Wissen um die Geschichte war entscheidend für den Erfolg der Bundesrepublik.

Daß Menschen eine zutreffende Darstellung ihrer Geschichte benötigen, um daraus zu lernen, habe ich bereits erwähnt. Die Internationalisierung der deutschen Geschichte hat dazu beigetragen. Welche Varianten des Lernens stellen wir fest? Und wie hat die Bundesrepublik davon profitiert? Zwei Arten sind meines Erachtens besonders relevant:

Die erste ist das Lernen aus der Vergangenheit, das bewußt und vorsätzlich erfolgt, um Anleitungen für eine andere Zukunft zu erhalten. Ein klassisches Beispiel dafür ist der Aufbau des politischen Systems der Bundesrepublik. Tragende Teile dieses Systems wurden von seinen Gründern entwickelt, um ein Wiederaufkommen des Nazismus zu verhindern. Das bedeutete unter anderem, die institutionellen Schwächen von Weimar zu vermeiden.

Eine zweite Art des Lernens vollzieht sich weniger bewußt und zielgerichtet. Menschen überdenken Überzeugungen und Wertvorstellungen anhand ihrer Erfahrungen und im Lichte konkurrierender Überzeugungen und Werte. Dies tun alle und täglich. Manchmal macht die große Mehrheit einer Gesellschaft die gleiche fundamentale Erfahrung und lernt auf diese Weise das gleiche. Das passiert typischerweise nach einem nationalen Trauma oder wenn grundlegende Institutionen der Gesellschaft Veränderungen durchlaufen. Als Beispiele, neben Deutschland: Japan wandelte nach dem Zweiten Weltkrieg seine ausgeprägt militaristische Kultur in eine mit stark pazifistischer Komponente. Und die Weißen im Süden der USA änderten nach der Abschaffung der gesetzlichen Rassentrennung ihre Einstellung zur Rolle der Schwarzen in der Gesellschaft grundlegend.

Solche Lernprozesse erfolgen weder automatisch noch über Nacht, sondern nach und nach. Was die Bundesrepublik betrifft, lag die wichtige Lernphase vorwiegend in den ersten Nachkriegsjahrzehnten. Ich meine die De-

tization and also, though more slowly and less completely, to its citizens' views of Jews. (I am surprised that, during the last year, so many people have objected to the notion that learning has taken place in the Federal Republic regarding Jews, especially since the evidence, including survey data, is overwhelming that it has.)

A proper understanding of German national history does not provide an unambiguous blueprint for the future. The past can never do that. But it can open future possibilities. It does so by clarifying the dangers that inhere in certain beliefs, practices, and institutions, and by providing powerful negative models that people conclude must not be repeated.

This is what a proper understanding, the internationalized understanding, of German national history furnished for the builders of the Federal Republic, who were at once certain prominent individuals, groups of elites, and, let us not forget, that portion of the German people who found themselves in the west. The more or less inescapable conclusion that followed from the dominant framework – that held the Holocaust to be the central event of modern German history and its cause to be the failure of democratic values and democratic institutions in Germany – was rightly understood to be that the only future for Germany is one firmly anchored in democratic values and institutions, and therefore bound to the western community of nations which, however imperfectly, lives by them.

Germans learned well from their history. Because so many drew the right conclusions, it has made it easier for this dual process of internationalization to go forward in Germany. After all, it was not just other countries that have wanted to bind Germany in the western institutions of the European Union and NATO. Many Germans have seen these institutions as a means of preventing any recurrence of the past by creating a set of institutional constraints and incentives for maintaining the political orientation of the Federal Republic.

Some might think that it is a shame, perhaps even Germany's shame, that the Federal Republic has lived and continues to live looking over its shoul-

mokratisierung und – obgleich langsamer und unvollständiger – die Einstellung der Bevölkerung zu den Juden. (In diesem Zusammenhang angemerkt: Mich hat überrascht, wieviele Deutsche während des letzten Jahres der Feststellung widersprachen, daß in der Bundesrepublik ein Lernprozeß das Verhältnis den Juden gegenüber stattgefunden hat. Dabei gibt es entsprechende Belege, Umfragen eingeschlossen, in überwältigender Zahl.)

Das richtige Verständnis der deutschen Nationalgeschichte liefert noch keinen eindeutigen Entwurf für die Zukunft. Geschichte kann das nie. Aber sie kann Möglichkeiten für die Zukunft eröffnen – indem sie Gefahren deutlich macht, welche bestimmte Überzeugungen, Handlungen und Institutionen in sich bergen, und indem sie abschreckende Beispiele liefert, welche die Menschen davon überzeugen, daß dergleichen sich nicht wiederholen darf.

Das hat ein angemessenes, das heißt internationalisiertes Verständnis deutscher Nationalgeschichte den Begründern der Bundesrepublik mitgegeben – herausragende Persönlichkeiten, Teile der Eliten und, nicht zu vergessen, jene Mehrheit der Bevölkerung, die sich im Westen wiederfand. Die mehr oder weniger zwangsläufige Schlußfolgerung, die dem vorherrschenden Rahmen folgt – daß nämlich der Holocaust das zentrale Ereignis der modernen deutschen Geschichte ist und im Scheitern der demokratischen Werte und Institutionen seine Ursache hat – diese Schlußfolgerung bestand darin, Deutschlands Zukunft in einer festen Verankerung demokratischer Werte und Institutionen zu sehen und daher in einer Bindung an die westliche Staatengemeinschaft, die sich, wie unvollkommen auch immer, an diesen Werten orientiert.

Deutsche haben viel aus der Geschichte gelernt. Weil so viele die richtigen Schlüsse gezogen haben, konnte die duale Internationalisierung leichter voranschreiten. Letzten Endes waren es nicht nur andere Länder, die Deutschland in die westlichen Institutionen, in Europäische Union und NATO einbinden wollten. Auch viele Deutsche sehen darin ein Mittel, das eine Wiederholung der Vergangenheit ausschließt.

Vielleicht denken heute manche, daß es der Bundesrepublik nicht mehr ansteht oder sogar zu ihrem Schaden ist, sich ständig nach den anderen um-

der in a manner unmatched by others and, in their view, unbefitting a country of its power and stature. They are wrong. It is precisely the opposite. The Federal Republic's political practice should be a source of satisfaction. Its mode of political activity, which has been a constituent feature of German democracy, has been an undeniable strength of the Federal Republic that should be understood, applauded, encouraged, and furthered by Germans and non-Germans alike.

The Federal Republic of Germany – and other countries – ought to be judged not according to some nationalist, that is to say, egoistic benchmark but according to a universal standpoint and standard. It ought to be assessed realistically compared to other countries. Comparatively, the Federal Republic, as I have already said, looks good. Its honesty regarding its past, the development of its democracy, and its conduct internationally have, whatever the flaws, been better than most and in some ways exemplary.

To the extent that internationalization has facilitated this, it should be a source not of distemper but of satisfaction in the Federal Republic. But satisfaction should not lead to complacency. As fine as the Federal Republic's record has been, the task of constructing an accurate national history and a responsible democracy is not and can never be finished, because it is forever ongoing. The Federal Republic should move still further down the path of internationalization that it has already set out.

It should be recognized, for example, that there are still aspects of the Nazi period which have never been fully discussed and victims which have received insufficient acknowledgment and no recompense. This includes many Jews and also members of other victim groups, such as homosexuals, the Sinti and Roma peoples, and millions of other Europeans whom Germans over fifty years ago killed or enslaved. Acknowledging the past does not shame today's Germany but makes emphatic to the whole world that the Federal Republic is different, and that it abhors such deeds and the beliefs which led to them.

I say this in part to underscore that no one should understand my appreciation for the genuine, enormous achievements of the Federal

zudrehen; daß das einem so mächtigen und großen Land unangemessen und sonst nirgendwo anzutreffen sei. Sie liegen falsch. Exakt das Gegenteil ist der Fall. Das politische Verhalten der Bundesrepublik sollte Anlaß zur Genugtuung geben. Ihre Art, Politik zu machen, ist ein festes Merkmal der deutschen Demokratie, eine unleugbare Stärke des Landes. Deutsche und Nichtdeutsche sollten das gleichermaßen verstehen, begrüßen, ermutigen und fördern.

Die Bundesrepublik Deutschland – und andere Länder – sollten nicht nach nationalistischen, also egoistischen Maßstäben beurteilt werden, sondern aus einem universellen Blickwinkel und mit universellen Standards. Die Bundesrepublik gilt es, realistisch im Vergleich zu anderen Ländern zu bewerten. Dabei schneidet das Land, ich habe es bereits gesagt, gut ab. Die Ehrlichkeit im Umgang mit der Vergangenheit, die Entwicklung der Demokratie und das Verhalten auf internationaler Ebene ist – ungeachtet aller Mängel – besser als in vielen anderen Ländern, in mancher Hinsicht sogar beispielhaft.

In dem Maße, wie die Internationalisierung dazu beigetragen hat, sollte sie in der Bundesrepublik nicht Anlaß für Unzufriedenheit, sondern zur Zufriedenheit sein. Doch diese Befriedigung darüber darf nicht zu Selbstzufriedenheit führen. Wie bemerkenswert die Leistungen der Bundesrepublik auch sein mögen – die Aufgaben, eine angemessene Nationalgeschichte zu schreiben und eine verantwortungsbewußte Demokratie zu gestalten, sind nie abgeschlossen, dies ist ein immerwährender Prozeß. Die Bundesrepublik sollte dem beschrittenen Weg der Internationalisierung weiter folgen.

Übersehen wir nicht: Es gibt immer noch Aspekte der Nazi-Zeit, die nie angemessen erörtert wurden. Und es gibt immer noch Opfer, die noch keine angemessene Anerkennung und keine Entschädigung erhalten haben. Neben vielen Juden zählen dazu Angehörige anderer Gruppen: Homosexuelle, Sinti und Roma und Millionen anderer Europäer, die vor über 50 Jahren von Deutschen getötet oder versklavt wurden. Sich dieser Vergangenheit zu stellen, bedeutet für das heutige Deutschland keine Schande. Es unterstreicht vielmehr gegenüber aller Welt, daß die Bundesrepublik anders ist – daß sie solche Taten und die Überzeugungen, die sie hervorbrachten, verabscheut.

Ich sage dies auch, damit niemand meine Anerkennung der außerordentlichen Errungenschaften der Bundesrepublik dahingehend versteht, daß

Republic to imply that a Schlußstrich (an end point) can now be drawn. The self-defeating strategy of a Schlußstrich calls to mind an observation by de Tocqueville: "As the past has ceased to throw its light upon the future, the mind of man wanders in obscurity." Putting this past behind – in the only important sense in which it can be kept at arm's length, of making sure that its does not become the basis for creating a future in its own image – can be done only by keeping it alive in people's minds. When one wanders in obscurity, there is no telling where one might end up.

Still, the Federal Republic's achievements are great and with respect to this mode of cultural and political practice, the Federal Republic should be a model for other countries. All countries would benefit from greater internationalization in the two ways that I have discussed. The external perspectives of others correct, at least somewhat, for two of the nation state's greatest failings: its tendency to glorify itself, for which national history is a critical component, and its drive to pursue its own self-understood interests even to the enormous detriment of others. All national histories should be internationalized. All democracies, all democratic elites in particular, should be induced to care more about how other nations view their actions.

It would be too much to expect, and perhaps not even desirable, that all states and peoples adopt a cosmopolitan perspective, namely a perspective that is not rooted in anything particular to that country. Yet it is possible for states and peoples to adopt more of an international pluralized perspective, namely a perspective that admits and grapples with the viewpoints of others. Outside perspectives, in this case, are almost inevitably critical perspectives that, if taken seriously, compel a people to reassess, and then justify or alter their own views and practices.

My book focuses exclusively on the past. My task, as I understood it, was to illuminate why and how the Holocaust occurred and unfolded as it did. My task was, therefore, not to render moral judgment but to explain why things happened. For this to be possible, it seemed to me that a shift in perspective was necessary. The long-standing focus on abstract institutions and structures – like the Nazi Party, the

nun ein Schlußstrich gezogen werden könnte. Die zum Scheitern verurteilte Strategie des „Schlußstrichs" ruft eine Bemerkung Tocquevilles in Erinnerung: „Seit die Vergangenheit nicht mehr ihr Licht auf die Zukunft wirft, wandert der menschliche Geist in Dunkelheit." Die Vergangenheit hinter sich zu lassen, ist ausschließlich in einem Sinne möglich: sie auf Abstand zu halten, um sicher zu gehen, daß sie nicht zu einer nach dem Bild dieser Vergangenheit geschaffenen Zukunft wird. Das aber kann nur heißen, die Vergangenheit in den Köpfen lebendig zu erhalten. Wer in der Dunkelheit wandert, weiß nicht, wohin er gerät.

Was in der Bundesrepublik erreicht wurde, ist von großem Gewicht und, im Hinblick auf die beschriebene kulturelle und politische Praxis, durchaus als Leitbild zu empfehlen. Alle Länder würden von einer breiteren Internationalisierung – in beiden erläuterten Arten – profitieren. Externe Sichtweisen korrigieren zumindest zum Teil zwei der größten Fehler des Nationalstaates: zum einen seine Tendenz zur Sebstverherrlichung, wobei viel von der Nationalgeschichte abhängt; zum anderen den Drang, dem zu folgen, was er als die eigenen Interessen begreift, auch wenn anderen daraus erhebliche Nachteile erwachsen. Die Nationalgeschichte eines jeden Landes sollte internationalisiert werden. Und alle Demokratien, vor allem deren Eliten, sollten dazu bewegt werden, sich öfter zu fragen, wie andere Nationen ihr Handeln bewerten.

Es wäre zuviel verlangt und vielleicht nicht einmal wünschenswert, daß alle Staaten eine kosmopolitische Sichtweise annehmen, eine Sichtweise also, die nicht in Eigenarten des jeweiligen Landes verwurzelt ist. Staaten und Völker können jedoch mehr von einer internationalen, pluralistischen Sichtweise übernehmen, die offen ist für den Standpunkt anderer und sich mit ihm auseinandersetzt. Externe Standpunkte sind in diesem Fall fast zwangsläufig kritische. Und sie zwingen, sofern enrstgenommen, ein Volk dazu, Ansichten und Handlungen neu zu bewerten und sie dann zu rechtfertigen oder zu ändern.

Mein Buch konzentriert sich ausschließlich auf die Vergangenheit. Die Aufgabe bestand darin aufzuzeigen, warum und wie der Holocaust sich ereignet hat. Nicht ein moralisches Urteil abzugeben war das Ziel, sondern zu erklären, warum Dinge geschehen sind. Dazu schien mir eine Verlagerung des Blickwinkels notwendig. Die schon lange bestehende Konzentration auf Institutionen und Strukturen – Nazi-Partei, SS, der

SS, and the terror apparatus – had to be replaced by one that put at the center of our inquiry and interpretation the human beings who contributed, however they did, to bringing the Holocaust about, which includes the actors' understanding of their deeds.

Since my book's publication, I have come to realize that my book is not just about the past. The enormous discussion that it has produced, especially here in Germany, has led me to understand ever more that the book is relevant to the future. Much of what I have said this evening attempts to explain why this is so. By helping to produce a discussion that both reinforces and augments the basic framework of understanding for German national history, my work seems to have reminded people that there is no usable German political model prior to the Federal Republic that is to be recaptured, which can serve as a model for the future. The democratic principles, the western anchor, the internationalizing orientation of the Federal Republic are, and must remain, its strengths.

By understanding what happened in Germany during the Nazi period – which entailed a thoroughgoing rejection of the enlightenment image of humanity and of the democratic political values and institutions that have governed the Federal Republic – by understanding what this rejection produced in Germany and Europe, a catastrophe unmatched in modern European history, for Jews, for Sintis and Romas, for Communists and Socialists, for the mentally ill, for homosexuals, for Poles, Ukrainians, Russians and other Europeans, and ultimately for the German people itself, by understanding why so many ordinary people lent their bodies and souls to producing this catastrophe, it becomes less likely that old forms will appeal to people today.

Versions of a mythical and sanitized past have, at times, found currency in Germany since 1945. Some attempts to "normalize" Germany's past would have had produced such an outcome. The "Historikerstreit" was fought over this terrain. Recent protests against the Hamburg Institute for Social Research's Wehrmacht exhibit reveal continuing resistance to facing basic truths. Mythologizing and sanitizing construc-

Terrorapparat – mußte ersetzt werden. Es sollten jene Menschen in den Mittelpunkt gerückt werden, die – auf welche Art auch immer – dazu beigetragen haben, daß der Holocaust geschehen konnte. Dazu gehört auch das Verständnis der Akteure von dem, was sie taten.

Seit der Veröffentlichung des Buches bin ich zu der Erkenntnis gelangt, daß es nicht nur von der Vergangenheit handelt. Die breite Diskussion, die es vor allem hier in Deutschland angeregt hat, macht mir immer mehr bewußt, daß das Buch auch die Zukunft betrifft. Ein Großteil dessen, was ich heute abend gesagt habe,versuchte zu erklären, warum das so ist. Indem es eine Diskussion ausgelöst hat, die den Rahmen des Verständnisses der deutschen Nationalgeschichte sowohl verstärkt als auch ergänzt, scheint mein Buch die Menschen an etwas erinnert zu haben: Vor der Bundesrepublik existierte in Deutschland kein politisches Modell, das wiederhergestellt werden und als Vorbild für die Zukunft dienen könnte. Die demokratischen Prinzipien, die Westverankerung und die internationalisierte Orientierung sind die Stärken der Bundesrepublik, und das sollte so bleiben.

Wenn man versteht, was während der Nazi-Zeit in Deutschland passierte – einschließlich der durchgehenden Ablehnung der Humanität im Sinne der Aufklärung und der demokratischen politischen Werte und Institutionen, die später für die Bundesrepublik grundlegend waren; wenn man versteht, wohin diese Ablehnung Deutschland und Europa führte, nämlich in die schlimmste Katastrophe der modernen europäischen Geschichte – für Juden, Sinti und Roma, Kommunisten, Sozialisten, für geistig Behinderte, Homosexuelle, Polen, Ukrainer, Russen und andere Europäer und schließlich für das deutsche Volk selbst; wenn man versteht, warum so viele normale Bürger mit Leib und Seele dazu beitrugen, daß diese Katastrophe geschehen konnte, dann sinkt die Wahrscheinlichkeit, daß Schemen der Vergangenheit die Menschen von heute erneut in ihren Bann ziehen könnten.

Verschiedene Versionen einer mythischen und bereinigten Vergangenheit haben seit 1945 zeitweise Verbreitung in Deutschland gefunden. Einige Versuche, die deutsche Vergangenheit zu „normalisieren", hätten zu einem solchen Ergebnis führen können. Genau darüber wurde der „Historikerstreit" ausgetragen. Die Proteste der letzten Zeit gegen die Wehrmachtausstellung des Hamburger Instituts für Sozialforschung machen deutlich, daß noch im-

tions have not been buried for good. Yet I do believe that the discussion in Germany during the last year shows that they have become ever less plausible to ever more people.

This issue is of some moment. German power has grown. The unusual postwar constellation of German and of international politics that produced the Bonn Republic has come to an end. The restraints of the Cold War have dissolved. The nation-state's will to power stands against the tempering effects of the internationalization of Germans' self-image and of German democracy, as well as the continuing domestic and international institutional restraints upon German power.

Which will prevail? Now that German democracy, and therefore Germany, is "mature," is it time for the internationalization of German national history and of German democracy to end?

No. The successful groundwork that has been laid by the Bonn Republic, including its unusual self-understanding and politics, needs to be carried over to the Berlin Republic.

In this respect it is not the Federal Republic, but other countries, which should change. It is also time for this German model to be internationalized, time for other nations to emulate Germany in constructing their national histories and contemporary national self-understandings.

If I understand the „Blätter" correctly, it is its members' interest in the future – particularly in this issue – and their understanding of the relationship between illuminating, discussing, and learning from the past and creating a democratic future that has brought us here today. Their commitment to the principles that have governed the Federal Republic and also to this view of the relationship between learning from history and constructing a desirable future is one reason, among others, for inviting Jürgen Habermas and Jan Philipp Reemtsma to speak here. No one has been a more articulate and tireless public champion both of the principles of the Federal Republic and of this understanding of national history than

mer Widerstand gegen grundlegende Wahrheiten geleistet wird. Mythologisierungsversuche oder das Bemühen um eine nachträgliche Bereinigung des Geschehenen sind nach wie vor nicht aus der Welt. Die Diskussionen im vergangenen Jahr haben jedoch meines Erachtens gezeigt, daß beides für immer mehr Menschen immer weniger glaubwürdig wird.

Dieses Thema ist von aktueller Bedeutung. Deutschland ist mächtiger geworden. Die ungewöhnliche Nachkriegskonstellation der deutschen und der internationalen Politik, die die Bonner Republik hervorgebracht hat, besteht nicht mehr. Die Beschränkungen des Kalten Krieges sind weggefallen. Der Machtwille des Nationalstaates steht den mäßigenden Auswirkungen des internationalisierten deutschen Selbstbildes und der deutschen Demokratie gegenüber. Hinzu kommen fortwährende nationale und internationale institutionelle Beschränkungen deutscher Macht.

Was wird sich letztendlich durchsetzen? Ist die Zeit gekommen, die Internationalisierung der deutschen Nationalgeschichte und der deutschen Demokratie zu beenden – jetzt, da die Bundesrepublik Deutschland „erwachsen" geworden ist?

Nein. Die Grundlagen der Bonner Republik und ihres Erfolgs, darunter ihr außergewöhnliches Selbstverständnis und ihre außergewöhnliche politische Praxis, müssen auf die Berliner Republik übertragen werden.

Deshalb sollte sich nicht die Bundesrepublik, sondern sollten andere Länder sich wandeln. Es ist an der Zeit, dieses deutsche Modell zu internationalisieren. Es ist Zeit, daß andere Nationen der Bundesrepublik in Sachen Nationalgeschichtsschreibung und Selbstverständnis nacheifern.

Was uns heute hier auf Initiative der „Blätter" zusammengeführt hat, ist ihr Interesse an der Zukunft und am Verhältnis zwischen dem Lernen aus der Vergangenheit und dem Schaffen einer demokratischen Zukunft. Das Engagement der Zeitschrift für die Prinzipien der Bundesrepublik und für deren Einstellung, was das Lernen aus der Geschichte und die Schaffung einer wünschenswerten Zukunft anbelangt, veranlaßte die Redaktion der „Blätter", Jürgen Habermas und Jan Philipp Reemtsma als Sprecher einzuladen. Niemand ist ein so klarer und unermüdlicher Verfechter sowohl der Grundlagen der Bundesrepublik als auch dieses Verständnisses von Nationalgeschichte wie Jürgen Habermas. Keiner hat sich mutiger und engagier-

Jürgen Habermas. No one has been a more courageous and forceful proponent of presenting an unadorned, unsparing view of the past than has Jan Philipp Reemtsma. So I feel especially grateful, not only for their generous words, but also that they accepted the Blätter's invitation in the first place.

By awarding me its Democracy Prize, the „Blätter" has done me a great honor and given me a gift: a better understanding of the possibilities of my own work. For the honor and the gift, I thank you with my head and my heart.

That I am being so acknowledged in Germany for writing a book with the unsettling and painful content that mine has is the strongest testimony to everything that I have said this evening, to the character and the democratic promise of contemporary Germany, and to the fact that it is really all the people in Germany, responsible for making the Federal Republic the democratic country that it has become, who deserve this prize.

ter für die Darstellung einer ungeschminkten und schonungslosen Sicht der Vergangenheit eingesetzt als Jan Philipp Reemtsma. Daher bin ich Ihnen besonders dankbar – nicht nur für Ihre großzügigen Worte, sondern auch dafür, daß sie diese Einladung der „Blätter“ angenommen haben.

Mit der Auszeichnung des Demokratiepreises haben die „Blätter“ mir eine große Ehre erwiesen. Darüber hinaus haben sie mir ein Geschenk gemacht: Sie haben mir ein besseres Verständnis dessen ermöglicht, was meine Arbeit vermag. Für die Ehre und das Geschenk möchte ich mich bedanken – mit Herz und Verstand.

Daß ich in Deutschland für ein Buch mit solch verunsicherndem und schmerzvollem Inhalt ausgezeichnet werde, ist der eindrucksvollste Beleg für alles, was ich heute abend gesagt habe, für den Charakter und das demokratische Potential des heutigen Deutschland und für die Tatsache, daß vielmehr diejenigen, die die von mir hier charakterisierte Bundesrepublik möglich gemacht haben und ihre Grundprinzipien verfechten, diesen Preis verdient haben.

Übersetzung: Arthur Heinrich und Karl D. Bredthauer

Press Release

Recipient of Democracy Prize 1997: Daniel Goldhagen

In 1997, the Democracy Prize of the *Blaetter für deutsche und internationale Politik* [*Journal for German and International Politics*] and its supporters' association is awarded to Daniel Jonah Goldhagen, author of the book *Hitler's Willing Executioners* [German: *Hitlers willige Vollstrecker*]. Following the recommendation of the editors, the decision was made at the annual meeting of the supporters' association.

Because of the penetrating quality and the moral power of his presentation Daniel Goldhagen has greatly stirred the consciousness of the German public. This is especially important in the present period of transition that is shaping the transformation of the Bonn Republic to the Berlin Republic. He has thus substantially contributed to the sharpening of the public's understandig of the background and the limits to Germany's "normalization".

Daniel Goldhagen accepts the prize. Among other things, he writes in his acceptance letter to the editors of the Blaetter:

"I am delighted, thrilled, and, even more, honored and deeply moved to receive your Demokratiepreis, which I, of course accept with unqualified joy and gratitude. Of the many good things that have happened to me since the publication of the book, I can think of none that has been more significant.

When I wrote my book I believed that it was only about how to understand and think about the past. More and more, I have come to realize that the book is also about the present and the future. In ways I never envisaged, it seems to have affected people's lives and produced a discussion – not just in Germany but nowhere more than in Germany – of a range of issues that provides meaning to people and that informs how people believe that they should govern themselves. Receiving this prize confirms that this is still truer than I have yet imagined."

The Blaetter-Demokratiepreis is endowed with 10.000 DM. In 1990, it was awarded to the democracy movement of the GDR, represented by Baerbel Bohley und Wolfgang Ullmann, in Berlin's Bonhoeffer-Haus, where the *Runde Tisch* used to meet. The laudatory speech was given by Walter Jens.

On March 10, 1997, Daniel Goldhagen will receive the prize in Bonn's Beethovenhalle in the evening of March 10, 1997. Jürgen Habermas and Jan Philipp Reemtsma will deliver the "laudatios" (the speeches in praise of the recipient of the prize); the honoree will reply with an acceptance speech. The award ceremony will begin at 08:00 p.m.

Bonn, January 7, 1997

Pressemitteilung

Demokratiepreis 1997 an Daniel Goldhagen

Der Demokratiepreis der *Blätter für deutsche und internationale Politik* (Bonn) und des Blätter-Fördervereins geht 1997 an Daniel Jonah Goldhagen, Autor des Buches *Hitler's Willing Executioners* (dt. *Hitlers willige Vollstrecker*). Dies hat auf Vorschlag der Blätter-Redaktion die Jahresversammlung des Fördervereins beschlossen.

Aufgrund der Eindringlichkeit und der moralischen Kraft seiner Darstellung hat Daniel Goldhagen dem öffentlichen Bewußtsein in der Bundesrepublik Deutschland wesentliche Impulse gegeben – und dies in einer den Übergang von der Bonner zur Berliner Republik prägenden Zeit. Er hat so wesentlich dazu beigetragen, die Sensibilität für Hintergründe und Grenzen einer deutschen „Normalisierung" zu schärfen.

Daniel Goldhagen nimmt den Preis an. In seiner Antwort an die Blätter-Redaktion heißt es u.a.:

> „In bin zutiefst bewegt und fühle mich sehr geehrt, Ihren Demokratiepreis zu empfangen, den ich mit uneingeschränkter Freude und Dankbarkeit annehme. Unter den vielen guten Dingen, die mir seit dem Erscheinen meines Buches passiert sind, kann ich mir nichts Bedeutsameres vorstellen.
>
> Als ich mein Buch schrieb, glaubte ich, es handele nur von der Vergangenheit und vom rechten Umgang mit ihr. Seither ist mir immer deutlicher geworden, daß es auch Gegenwart und Zukunft betrifft. Ich hätte mir nie träumen lassen, wie sehr dies Buch Menschen in ihrem Selbstverständnis berühren und welche Diskussionen es auslösen würde – nicht nur in Deutschland, aber nirgendwo stärker als in Deutschland. Neben einer Reihe von Fragen, die den Menschen Sinn vermitteln, steht zur Debatte, wie man sich als Bürger verantwortlich verhalten sollte. Die Verleihung des Preises belegt nachdrücklich den Gegenwartsbezug des Buches."

Der Blätter-Demokratiepreis ist mit 10.000 DM dotiert. 1990 wurde er im Berliner Bonhoefferhaus, Tagungsstätte des „Runden Tisches", an die Demokratiebewegung der DDR, vertreten durch Bärbel Bohley und Wolfgang Ullmann, vergeben. Die Rede auf die Preisträger hielt Walter Jens.

Daniel Goldhagen nimmt den Preis am Abend des 10. März 1997 in der Bonner Beethovenhalle entgegen. Es sprechen Jürgen Habermas, Jan Philipp Reemtsma und der Preisträger selbst. Die Veranstaltung beginnt um 20 Uhr.

Bonn, 7. Januar 1997

Pressestimmen

„Ich bin nur ein Bote"

US-Autor Daniel Jonah Goldhagen, 38, über die positive Aufnahme seines Bestsellers „Hitlers willige Vollstrecker" in Deutschland. Für das Buch erhält er diesen Montag in Bonn den Demokratiepreis der „Blätter für deutsche und internationale Politik".

Spiegel: Jürgen Habermas und Jan Philipp Reemtsma halten Lobreden auf Sie. Haben Sie erwartet, daß Sie vom Unhold so rasch zum Helden würden?
Goldhagen: In diesem Ausmaß nicht. Daß meine Holocaust-Thesen Diskussionen auslösten, hat mich allerdings nicht überrascht. Viele, da war ich schon letzten Herbst sicher, würden das Buch wichtig finden, wenn sie es erst selbst lesen – und genauso war es.
Spiegel: Einige Bücher zu dieser neuen Vergangenheitsdebatte gibt es schon. Fühlen Sie sich als Geschichtslehrer der Deutschen?
Goldhagen: In der Debatte geht es gar nicht um mich – weder damals bei den Angriffen noch jetzt bei der Ehrung. Es geht darum, wie normale interessierte Menschen hier Fragen an die Vergangenheit stellen. Es geht um das Verstehen einer Epoche, um die Wahrheit. Ich bin nur ein Bote.
Spiegel: Sie haben eine heftige Debatte entfacht. Wollen Sie mit neuen Thesen zum Thema nachlegen?
Goldhagen: Ich habe eine Menge wissenschaftlicher Interessen. Als nächstes möchte ich eine vergleichende Studie über den Völkermord im 20. Jahrhundert schreiben ...
Spiegel: ... wobei Sie unweigerlich den ganzen Historikerstreit aufrollen müssen, aus dem das fatale Aufrechnen von Massenmorden noch in übler Erinnerung ist.

Goldhagen: Vergleichen an sich ist als Methode vollkommen legitim – solange es nicht bloß für politische Umwertungen benutzt wird, sondern wissenschaftlicher Aufklärung dient.
Spiegel: Läßt sich das so einfach trennen? Die Ehrung, die jetzt an Sie geht, liefert möglicherweise jenen Unbelehrbaren, die kürzlich in München wieder aufmarschierten, neue Vorwände.
Goldhagen: Ach, die wollen Politik machen. Das wird es immer geben. Mir geht es um historische Einsicht und darum, daß Leute von der Geschichte etwas lernen. Denn das kann sie auch zum Nachdenken anregen, welchen Prinzipien ihre eigene, heutige Gesellschaft folgen sollte. Solche Zukunftsfragen müssen natürlich hier, im vereinigten Deutschland, ausgiebig diskutiert werden.

In: „Der Spiegel", 11/1997

„Modell Deutschland"

Der Verfasser des umstrittenen Holocaust-Buches „Hitlers willige Vollstrecker", der amerikanische Wissenschaftler Daniel Jonah Goldhagen, hat den Deutschen bescheinigt, nach dem Krieg vorbildlich an die Vergangenheitsbewältigung und den Aufbau einer dauerhaften Demokratie herangegangen zu sein. Bei der Entgegennahme des Demokratiepreises der „Blätter für deutsche und internationale Politik" sprach Goldhagen vor über 2000 Zuhörern gestern abend in Bonn von einem „Modell Deutschland": Die Grundlagen der Bonner Republik müßten nicht nur auf die Berliner Republik, sondern auch auf andere Länder übertragen werden.

Die Bundesrepublik sah der Historiker gekennzeichnet von zwei überraschenden Entwicklungen: Zum einen habe sich eine Nationalgeschichte herausgebildet, in die kritische Perspektiven Außenstehender in-

tegriert worden seien. Dadurch hätten die Deutschen beschönigenden, mythologisierenden und selbsttäuschenden Tendenzen nationaler Geschichtsschreibung erfolgreich entgegenwirken können. Zum anderen betreffe die Internationalisierung auch den Aufbau der Nachkriegsdemokratie selbst – ja, Geschichtsverständnis und Demokratie hingen in wesentlichen Teilen zusammen. Goldhagen: „Die Entwicklung eines angemessenen Rahmens für die Sicht der Vergangenheit hat wesentlich zum Entstehen eines politischen Systems verantwortungsbewußter Demokratie beigetragen."

Karlheinz Koppe, Vorsitzender des Blätter-Fördervereins, begrüßt Gäste und Teilnehmer der Preisverleihung. Foto: Josef Menzen

Nachdrücklich wandte sich der amerikanische Historiker dagegen, einen „Schlußstrich" zu ziehen. Diese Strategie sei zum Scheitern verurteilt. Die Vergangenheit hinter sich zu lassen, sei ausschließlich in einem Sinn möglich: „sie auf Abstand zu halten, um sicherzugehen, daß sie nicht zu einer nach dem Bild dieser Vergangenheit geschaffenen Zukunft wird." Das aber könne nur heißen, die Vergangenheit in den Köpfen lebendig zu erhalten. Goldhagen: „Wer in der Dunkelheit wandert, weiß nicht, wohin er gerät."

Der Demokratiepreis war zuvor 1990 in der Tagungsstätte des „Runden Tisches" an Bärbel Bohley und Wolfgang Ullmann, stellvertretend für die Demokratiebewegung der DDR, verliehen worden. Goldhagen erhielt die mit 10 000 Mark dotierte Auszeichnung, weil er wesentlich dazu beigetragen habe, „die Sensibilität für Hintergründe und Grenzen einer deutschen ‚Normalität' zu schärfen". Anläßlich der Verleihung sagte der Soziologe Jürgen Habermas gestern abend, Goldhagens Untersuchungen seien genau auf die Fragen zugeschnitten gewesen, die private

wie öffentliche Diskussionen seit einem halben Jahrhundert polarisiert hätten: War der „Zivilisationsbruch“ eher wie ein Naturereignis und ist daher aus den Umständen zu erklären, oder muß man ihn verantwortlich handelnden Personen zuschreiben? Der Förderer der Sozialforschung, Jan Phillip Reemtsma, würdigte das Holocaust-Buch als nicht mehr wegzudenkenden Beitrag zur Bereitschaft, „sich dem tatsächlichen Geschehen zu stellen und sich damit abzufinden“.

Wie Goldhagen vor der Preisverleihung gegenüber Journalisten ergänzend erläutert hatte, ist für ihn die Nachkriegsentwicklung Deutschlands auch deshalb ein „sehr hoffnungsvolles Modell“, da sich hier gezeigt habe, daß nicht nur der einzelne, sondern auch eine ganze Gesellschaft lernfähig sei und sich durch Lernen verändern könne. Auf Nachfragen ging Goldhagen ebenfalls auf die aktuellen Proteste gegen die Ausstellung „Verbrechen der Wehrmacht“ in München ein. Er warnte davor, denjenigen zuviel Aufmerksamkeit zu widmen, die zuwenig aus der Geschichte gelernt hätten. Für ihn sei es vielmehr bemerkenswert, wie enorm die Öffentlichkeit an der Ausstellung interessiert ist, die schon bis Ende 1998 ausgebucht sei.

Gregor Mayntz, in: „Rheinische Post“, 11.3.1997

Bestseller nach Kritik

„Ich kenne kein anderes Land, das so offen und konsequent mit den unrühmlichen und schrecklichen Kapiteln der eigenen Vergangenheit umgeht.“ Der junge amerikanische Historiker Daniel Goldhagen schlug gestern bei der Verleihung des „Demokratiepreises“ einer renommierten politischen Zeitschrift des linken Spektrums versöhnliche Töne an. Denn bislang war ihm nicht der Ruf vorausgeeilt, es besonders gut mit den Deutschen zu meinen.

Gerade Historiker hatten ihm vorgeworfen, unter dem Vorwand der Wissenschaftlichkeit ein Buch über den Nationalsozialismus geschrieben zu haben, das die Belebung der längst überholt geglaubten Kollektivschuldthese zur Folge haben könne. Aus persönlicher Betroffenheit habe Goldhagen die Historikermaxime, sich „sine ira et studio" – ohne Zorn und Eifer – einem Thema zu nähern, über Bord geworfen. Die vorgelegten Fakten seien zwar im Detail neu – nicht jedoch seine überspitzt herausgearbeitete These über die Beteiligung d e r Deutschen am Holocaust.

Geschadet hat ihm die Kritik einiger Fachleute nicht. Es gelang Goldhagen, worum viele Zunftkollegen ihn beneiden: Seine 700seitige Doktorarbeit „Hitlers willige Vollstrecker" wurde zum Bestseller. Unter den Menschen ist das Bedürfnis nach Auseinandersetzung mit dem schrecklichsten Kapitel deutscher Geschichte offenbar ungebrochen.

Goldhagens These geht von der Verantwortung des einzelnen auch in der totalitären Diktatur aus. Die Deutschen unter Hitler seien keine willenlosen Rädchen in einer automatenhaft funktionierenden Maschinerie gewesen. Sollte die Langzeitwirkung Goldhagens darin bestehen, die Diskussion über diese Problematik in breiteste Schichten getragen zu haben, dann ist dies das Schlechteste nicht.

Christian Striefler, in: „Sächsische Zeitung", 11.3.1997

Lob von Goldhagen

Wer bisher Daniel Goldhagen für einen Pauschalisten gehalten hat – jenen US-Autor, der die Deutschen vermeintlich in ihrer Gesamtheit für die Nazi-Verbrechen verantwortlich macht – dem dürften die jüngsten Bemerkungen Goldhagens Anlaß geben, sein Urteil zu überdenken: Das Deutschland des Jahres 1997, so stellte der Autor des Bestsellers „Hitlers willige Vollstrecker" in einem Vortrag anerkennend fest, sei ein „Demokratie-Modell" mit weltweiter Ausstrahlung. Goldhagen sieht in der Bundesrepublik einen „international verantwortungsvoll agierenden

Das Rimsky-Korsakow-Quartett aus St. Petersburg spielte Werke von Dmitri Schostakowitsch und Viktor Ullmann. *Foto: Josef Menzen*

Nationalstaat". Und ihren Bürgern bescheinigt er, daß sie fähig sind, die richtigen Lehren aus der Geschichte zu ziehen.

Spricht so ein Pauschalist, ein Vereinfacher? Wohl kaum. Bemerkenswert ist auch seine Beobachtung, daß die Rolle der Rechtsextremisten häufig überbewertet wird – besonders, da die Bilder des Aufmarsches von Jung-Nazis vor der Wehrmacht-Ausstellung in München noch in frischer Erinnerung sind. Aber Goldhagen hat Recht: Die Demokratie hierzulande ist gefestigt genug, auch mit diesen Erscheinungen angemessen umzugehen.

Nach dem Urteil des amerikanischen Soziologen setzt sich kaum ein Land so intensiv mit den dunklen Seiten seiner Geschichte auseinander. Das ist eine Anerkennung nicht nur für die Zunft der Historiker. Verfehlt wäre es aber, daraus den Schluß zu ziehen, die Beschäftigung mit der Vergangenheit nun ruhen zu lassen. Die demokratische Erfolgsgeschichte in der Bundesrepublik basiert wesentlich auf Impulsen von außen. Auch auf solch umstrittenen Büchern wie dem Goldhagens.

Jan Sellner, in: „Stuttgarter Nachrichten", 11.3.1997

Heraus aus der Gefahr des historischen Vernebelns?

Die Aktion ist nicht ohne Geschick. Ein feines, aber nach wie vor kleines Monatsheft, die *Blätter für deutsche und internationale Politik*, loben einen Demokratiepreis aus, erkennen ihn Daniel Jonah Goldhagen zu, jenem jungen Amerikaner, der im vergangenen Jahr mit seinem Buch über „Hitlers willige Vollstrecker" die kritische Intelligenz in Aufruhr und Debatten gestürzt hat. Und alle kommen.

Mehr als 2000 Geladene finden sich in der Bonner Beethovenhalle ein, ergraute Altlinke sind darunter, manche Jüngere, in jedem Fall viele, die einst der Vision des demokratischen Sozialismus nachspürten. Mit Sorgfalt getroffen ist auch die Auswahl der Preis-Redner: Der eine, Jürgen Habermas, hat vor zehn Jahren im Historikerstreit mitgefochten, der andere, Jan Philipp Reemtsma, ist Mitinitiator jener Wehrmachtsausstellung, die in diesen Monaten in verschiedenen deutschen Städten (derzeit in München) zu sehen ist.

Kein Zweifel, das Thema hat Konjunktur. Die Klemperer-Tagebücher, das Goldhagen-Werk, die Ausstellung, in der die Verbrechen der Wehrmacht dokumentiert sind, man könnte den Film „Schindlers Liste" hinzufügen: Offensichtlich gibt es eine neue Bereitschaft der Deutschen, sich der Frage zu stellen, „wie tief der Konsens von Regime und Bevölkerung" (Reemtsma) gewesen ist, eine verbrecherische Politik nicht nur zu formulieren, sondern auch zu exekutieren. Offensichtlich gibt es ein kollektives Bedürfnis, die historischen Horizonte zu weiten, die sich bei der Frage nach den tieferen Ursachen für den Holocaust bisher im wesentlichen auf die Betrachtung der gesellschaftlichen Eliten beschränkte. Offensichtlich ist eine neue gesellschaftliche Bereitschaft vorhanden, den Kreis derjenigen, die zur Mittäterschaft bereit waren, erheblich auszudehnen.

Lange Zeit, so Reemtsmas These, habe die „Metapher von der industriellen Vernichtung", der Verweis auf das Unvorstellbare von der Auseinandersetzung abgehalten. Die „Entlastung durch das Extrem" nennt der Gründer des Hamburger Instituts für Sozialforschung diese Form

des Ausweichens und mutmaßt eine „spezifisch deutsche Verleugnungsdynamik“. Eingerahmt werde diese Form des Leugnens von einem „bis heute nicht zureichenden Verständnis der Gewaltdynamik selbst“. Die säuberliche Aufteilung des Tötens in Vernichtungslagern zum einen und des Tötens in Ausübung des gewöhnlichen Kriegshandwerks zum andern berge die Gefahr des Vernebelns in sich. Für KZ-Schlächter wie für Wehrmachtssoldaten gelte gleichermaßen: Der Holocaust hat sich letzten Endes deshalb ereignet, weil „auf einfachster Ebene gesehen einzelne Menschen über einen längeren Zeitraum hinweg andere Menschen zu Abertausenden umgebracht haben“.

Distanz zum eigenen Tun, diese „kritische Einstellung gegenüber Eigenem“, die Goldhagen gefördert habe, findet auch den Beifall von Jürgen Habermas. Tief hat er sich ins Private zurückgezogen und um das Goldhagen-Buch und die daran anknüpfende Debatte einen weiten Bogen geschlagen. Nun meldet er sich in Bonn doch zu Wort. Unveränderlich wäre das Undenkbare nicht gewesen, sagt er. Der Antisemitismus sei vom stillschweigenden Einverständnis breiter Schichten der Bevölkerung getragen worden. Mehr noch: Er, der sich stets geweigert hat, den Holocaust als eine Art Betriebsunfall der deutschen Geschichte zu interpretieren, glaubt: „Die Täter lebten in einer Welt, in der Nachdenklichkeit, Diskussion und Auseinandersetzung möglich waren.“ Deshalb beziehe sich der eigentliche Verdienst Goldhagens auf spezifische Überlieferungen und Mentalitäten, auf Denk- und Wahrnehmungsweisen eines bestimmten, kulturellen Kontextes. „Sie bezieht sich nicht auf ein Unveränderliches, in das wir uns zu schicken haben, sondern auf Faktoren, die durch einen Bewußtseinswandel verändert werden können.“

Und der Preisträger selbst? Der betrachtet nach Abschluß seiner Arbeit und der kraftraubenden anschließenden Debatte manches anders. Differenzierter. Und merklich wohlwollender. Oder hat es mit der Aura der Preisverleihung zu tun? Jedenfalls bekundet er: „Ich kenne kein Land, das so offen und konsequent mit den unrühmlichen und schrecklichen Kapiteln der eigenen Vergangenheit umgeht.“ Gewiß, da sei der Druck des Auslands gewesen. Mehr als anderswo hätten die Sichtweisen Außenstehender die Entscheidungsprozesse der Politik beeinflußt. Und doch

gebe es Anlaß zu Genugtuung: „Das Wissen um die Geschichte war entscheidend für den Erfolg der Bundesrepublik.“ Und: „Deutsche haben viel aus der Geschichte gelernt.“

Horand Knaup, in: „Badische Zeitung“ 12.3.1997

Der lange Schrecken

„Warum glaubt ihr nicht euren Vätern?“ Die seltsame Frage steht auf einem Schild, mit dem ein alter Mann vor der Bonner Beethovenhalle ausharrt. Die meisten Gäste schenken ihm keine Beachtung. Goldhagens Publikum ist jung. Ohne Frage gehört es zur Generation der Enkel der Täter, von denen sein Buch handelt. Ein paar Ältere sind allerdings auch da, in der Halle und draußen auf dem Vorplatz. Die in der Halle zeigen Sympathie für Goldhagen und applaudieren seinen Laudatoren. Für die da draußen hat der Krieg kein Ende: „Warum glaubt ihr nicht euren Vätern?“ Es könnte das Motto des Abends sein.

Daniel Jonah Goldhagen in Deutschland, dritte Runde. Nach den ersten Diskussionen über sein Buch im letzten Frühjahr, nach dem Bestseller-Erfolg in Deutschland und der triumphalen Tournee im Herbst kehrt Goldhagen jetzt zurück, um sich in aller Form preisen zu lassen. Die „Blätter für deutsche und internationale Politik“ haben ihm den „Demokratiepreis 1997“ zugesprochen. Zuletzt erhielten ihn, im Jahr 1990, die Bürgerrechtler der untergegangenen DDR, vertreten durch Wolfgang Ullmann und Bärbel Bohley. Goldhagen, so die Begründung, habe „aufgrund der Eindringlichkeit und der moralischen Kraft seiner Darstellung dem öffentlichen Bewußtsein in der Bundesrepublik Deutschland, wesentliche Impulse gegeben“. In einer kritischen Zeit der deutschen Politik habe er „wesentlich dazu beigetragen, die Sensibilität für Hintergründe und Grenzen einer deutschen ‚Normalisierung‘ zu schärfen“. Das ist wesentlich gesprochen.

Daniel Jonah Goldhagen ist zu loben. Der Aufgabe unterziehen sich an diesem Abend Jürgen Habermas und Jan Philipp Reemtsma. Alle drei betätigen sich als Zeithistoriker, ohne Historiker zu sein. Der amerikanische Politologe ist es sowenig wie der deutsche Sozialphilosoph oder der Literaturwissenschaftler aus Hamburg. Goldhagen, Habermas und Reemtsma sind Meister in der Kunst, Streit über die Geschichte zu entfachen, drei Meister des historischen Diskurses in der Medienöffentlichkeit – nicht aber drei Historiker. An diesem Abend wiegt das noch geringer als sonst. Nicht Goldhagens Beitrag zur historischen Forschung ist zu loben, sondern die Wirkung, die sein Buch in der deutschen Öffentlichkeit getan hat. Und von öffentlicher Wirkung verstehen die drei Redner viel.

Die historische Fachwelt hat Goldhagen so ziemlich alle Vorwürfe gemacht, die geeignet sind, die wissenschaftliche Reputation eines Zeithistorikers zu zerstören. Man hat ihm Vernachlässigung wesentlicher Quellen vorgeworfen, Einseitigkeiten in der Auswahl und Deutung, die unseriöse Ausbeutung von Pionierarbeiten wie der von Christopher Browning, reduktionistische Erklärungsmodelle und stilistische Taktlosigkeiten.

Man hat ihm vorgeworfen, die Deutschen ins mentale Gefängnis des antisemitischen Zwangscharakters zu werfen oder den Täter Hitler zu entlasten, indem er Millionen von Tätern anklagte. All das hat seinem Erfolg nichts angehabt.

Goldhagen ist es gelungen, die Achse des historischen Diskurses umzudrehen. Lange Zeit hat sich die Erforschung der nationalsozialistischen Verbrechen auf den Massenmord in den Vernichtungslagern konzentriert. Für die Mommsen, Jäckel, Hillberg waren die Motive des Verbrechens irrational, die Ausführung hingegen planvoll, industriell. Goldhagen, der sich den individuell verübten Taten zuwendet, sieht rational aufklärbare, ideologische Motive – jetzt ist es die Ausführung, die irrational wird. Die Hintergründe des Verhaltens werden einsichtig: Prinzipiell sei alles erklärbar, hat Goldhagen kürzlich gesagt.

Schlagartig gelangt man so wieder zu einem gesicherten Weltbild. Der Einzelne, nach der bisherigen Forschung ein schwer zu beurteilendes

Rad in einer komplizierten, kafkaesken Maschinerie, wird wieder in einen Spielraum des Verhaltens gestellt. Mag dieser Spielraum auch begrenzt, mögen seine Motive ideologisch und böse sein, sein Handeln ist nicht länger völlig unfrei. Wer die Subjekte der Geschichte nach moralischen Kategorien beurteilen will, muß ihnen die elementare Freiheit, zu tun oder zu lassen, rückerstatten. Goldhagen hat die Geschichte wieder auf den Einzelnen gestellt. Mit dem Einzelnen kann man sich identifizieren, über ihn kann man Abscheu empfinden. Diesen Zugang zur Geschichte der NS-Verbrechen, einmal eröffnet, wird keine Fachhistorie jemals wieder zustellen. Wer Gertrud Himmelfarb nicht kennt und nie die Zeugnisliteratur des Holocaust gelesen hat, kann das als ein Verdienst Daniel Jonah Goldhagens ansehen.

Über Goldhagens Verdienste zu reden ist keine leichte Sache. Diese Erfahrung hat auch Jürgen Habermas machen müssen. Gewiß hat Goldhagen historiographische Verdienste: Die Erforschung und eindringliche Darstellung der Todesmärsche der letzten Kriegswochen gehört dazu. Aber darüber mag der „Nicht-Historiker" Habermas nicht reden. Er will über die positive Wirkung des Buches für das demokratische Bewußtsein in der Bundesrepublik sprechen. Für Habermas Routinesache: die Notwendigkeit historischer Aufklärung für die Achtung und Selbstachtung der Bürger. Die Probleme retrospektiver Zurechnung von Verbrechen, der Unterschied zwischen dem Juristen, der sich für die Vorwerfbarkeit von Handlungen interessiert, und dem Historiker, der sich um die Aufklärung von Ursachen bemüht. Daß Goldhagen diese Grenzlinie keinen Augenblick lang respektiert hat, läßt Habermas unerwähnt.

Lobenswert findet er an Goldhagens Buch insgesamt, daß es dem Wunsch „mancher Konservativer" nach fraglosen Traditionen zuwiderläuft. Im Detail fasziniert ihn, wie Goldhagen durch seine Fallstudien ein Bild von Tätern gewinnt, „die kein Unrechtsbewußtsein hatten", weil sie sich zur bösen Tat berechtigt glaubten. Doch die Überspitzung der Browningschen These von den „ganz normalen Männern" zu „ganz normalen Deutschen" verursacht Habermas Unbehagen, und dem Goldhagen, der die Judenvernichtung als „nationales Projekt der Deutschen" ansieht, widerspricht er mit dem konzessionsbereiten Goldhagen, der sich

in seinem – später verfaßten – Vorwort gegen monokausale Ansätze wendet. Da hält der Laudator Habermas das Opus des Demokratiepreisträgers nur noch mit ganz spitzen Fingern.

Karl D. Bredthauer, Daniel Goldhagen und Wolfgang Zellner (Blätter-Förderverein), der die Pressekonferenz leitete. *Foto: Damian Müller*

Jan Philipp Reemtsma kann mit dem medienwirksamen Zugpferd Goldhagen mehr anfangen. Er spannt es versuchsweise vor den eigenen Karren, und sieh, es zieht. Goldhagen habe fortgesetzt, was Spielberg mit „Schindlers Liste“ begonnen habe: Er habe die individuelle Verantwortung wieder zum Thema gemacht. So habe er das „merkwürdige Verständnis von Freiheit“ gebrochen, das nur die krasse Alternative von „Mittäterschaft“ und selbstmörderischem Widerstand zuließ. Daraus folgt eine fulminante Attacke auf die bisherige Zeitgeschichtsschreibung, die nie Freiheitsspielräume freigelegt, sondern immer nur Handlungszwänge bezeichnet habe. Von „Entlastung durch das Extrem“ ist die Rede, welche sich die einseitige Erforschung des industriellen Tötens verschafft habe, von „Verleugnung“, die auch den Diskurs der kritischen Historie geprägt habe.

Der Splitter im Auge der Geschichtsforschung entspricht dem Balken in der Vergangenheitswahrnehmung der Bundesrepublik, meint Reemtsma. Erst seit kurzem zeichne sich eine Wende ab: „Die Furcht vor der Betrachtung des Jedermann und der Möglichkeit, den eigenen Vater, Großvater oder Onkel, zuweilen die Tante oder die Mutter wiederzuerkennen, ist schließlich durch die Bereitschaft ersetzt worden, sich diesem Erkenntnisrisiko auszusetzen.“ Als Belege für diesen Gesinnungswandel nennt Reemtsma den Erfolg der Klemperer-Tagebücher, Goldhagens –

Buch und die von ihm initiierte Ausstellung über die Verbrechen der Wehrmacht.

Zweierlei Erziehung

Der Karren, vor den Reemtsma das Goldhagensche Erfolgswerk spannt, ist ein großes volkspädagogisches Unternehmen. Jan Philipp Reerntsma führt ein Werk fort, das in den Jahren nach ´68 steckenblieb und sich in politischen Zänkereien, im Lebensweltlichen und Ökologischen verlor: das Projekt einer rückhaltlosen Aufklärung der NS-Vergangenheit der Deutschen – jedes einzelnen Deutschen. Er will die Väter zwingen, das Wort zu sagen, das sie angeblich den Söhnen schulden; die Enkel aber will er mit sanfter Hand auf den rechten Weg leiten. Auch für ihn, das zeigt sein reicher Gebrauch von Termini der Psychoanalyse, bedeutet das Aussprechen des Unsäglichen die Möglichkeit der Katharsis. Doch die Zeiten sind nicht mehr wie in den fünfziger Jahren, als der bewunderte Arno Schmidt mit dem Zensor rang. In den neunziger Jahren droht die von Reemtsma betriebene Aufforderung zum Diskurs und zum Streit alles Gesagte in jenem „bodenlosen Gerede" aufgeben zu lassen, das er selbst erntete, als er Unternehmer um Spenden für die Gedenkstätte in Neuengamme bat.

Die Projekte Jan Philipp Reemtsmas und Daniel Jonah Goldhagens haben einen gemeinsamen Nenner. Es ist der Schrecken. Doch ihre Pädagogiken des Schreckens weisen Unterschiede auf. Reemtsma will seine Landsleute dazu zwingen, sich in den Schrecken zu vertiefen: „Der Schrecken sollte nachhaltig sein. Sonst stimmt das Sensorium nicht." Goldhagen hat den Schrecken längst hinter sich gelassen. Nach dem Inferno, das die ganz gewöhnlichen Deutschen angerichtet haben, haben sie jetzt, genauso gewöhnlich wie damals, nur ungewöhnlich gut belehrt durch ihre Freunde, das Paradies der exportfähigen Demokratie erreicht. Das „Modell Deutschland" hat Serienreife erlangt, bescheinigt Goldhagen in seiner Dankesrede. Da möchte man doch wieder den Vätern glauben.

Ulrich Raulff, in: „Frankfurter Allgemeine Zeitung", 12.3.1997

Was frühere Verbrechen für Bürger heute bedeuten

Fünf Jahrzehnte nach Kriegsende zeigen die neuen Debatten über die Verbrechen der Nazis für Jan Philipp Reemtsma, daß Deutsche heute bereit sind, „sich dem tatsächlich Geschehenen zu stellen". Dabei gehe es nicht vorwiegend „um Schuld oder Entschuldigung", fügte Jürgen Habermas am Montag abend in Bonn hinzu, sondern um „eine kritische Selbstvergewisserung der Nachkommen".

Seit zwei Jahren wandelt sich in der Öffentlichkeit die Sicht auf die Vergangenheit. Für die neue Perspektive nach dem Umbruch in Ostdeutschland und auf dem Weg in die „Berliner Republik" macht Reemtsma bei der Verleihung des Demokratiepreises an Daniel Goldhagen vor allem drei Impulse verantwortlich – der Vorstand des Hamburger Instituts für Sozialforschung nennt die Tagebücher des Victor Klemperer, die Studie Goldhagens über „Hitlers willige Vollstrecker" und die von seinem Institut verantwortete Ausstellung über die Verbrechen der deutschen Wehrmacht. Allesamt beschrieben sie den Teil des Genozids, der vor Auschwitz geschah.

Damit deutet Reemtsma auf eine Lücke und hebt hervor, daß der systematischen Vernichtung der Juden die zielgerichtete Ausgrenzung von 1933 an vorausgegangen war. Die Reaktionen auf die beiden Bücher und die Dokumentation der Verbrechen der deutschen Wehrmacht von 1941 an deuten für Reemtsma auch auf „die Bereitschaft" hin, „sich den dort aufgeworfenen Fragen zu stellen".

Dabei macht der stereotype Streit über die Wehrmachts-Ausstellung aber auch „den Gegensatz" deutlich, der für den Sozialphilosophen Habermas „seit den Anfängen der Bundesrepublik besteht": Möchten die einen „den Zivilisationsbruch", für den Auschwitz als Synonym steht, „lieber wie ein Naturereignis aus den Umständen erklären", schrieben die anderen die Verbrechen „verantwortlich handelnden Personen zu". So stehe der „Vorwurf der Verleugnung" dem „der selbstgerechten Morali-

sierung" gegenüber. Durch „diesen heillosen Streit", merkt Habermas in seiner Laudatio auf den von den „Blättern für deutsche und internationale Politik" gewürdigten Goldhagen an, werde aber die eigentliche Frage verdeckt: Welche Bedeutung hat denn die rückblickende „Zurechnung von Verbrechen, die wir heute zum Zweck einer ethisch-politischen Selbstverständigung unter Bürgern vornehmen?"

Habermas stemmt sich gegen die seit 1989 sich breitmachende „neue Sorte von vaterländischem Geist", die auf den im Historikerstreit vor zehn Jahren vorgetragenen Revisionismus aufbauen kann. Damals trat der Philosoph als Widersacher des Historikers Ernst Nolte auf. Heute hebt er in dem Zusammenhang von „politischem Selbstverständnis" und „historischem Bewußtsein" die Rolle des Bürgers hervor: Während die Enthüllungen von Verbrechen in den Familien „private Angelegenheiten" blieben, haben die Nachfahren „als Bürger ein öffentliches Interesse am dunkelsten Kapitel ihrer nationalen Geschichte" – für sich selbst und für „ihr Verhältnis zu den Opfern und deren Nachkommen".

So entsteht Habermas zufolge aus „einem weit verbreiteten individuell schuldhaften Verhalten in der Vergangenheit das Bewußtsein kollektiver Haftung". Das aber habe mit einer kollektiven Schuld nichts zu tun. Ein Gedanke, der auch der aufgeregten Debatte über die Wehrmachts-Ausstellung ganz guttun könnte.

Matthias Arning, in: „Frankfurter Rundschau", 12.3.1997

„Das Böse ist das verkehrte Gute"

„Die Bonner Beethoven-Halle ist voll – voller noch, als die Baupolizei erlaubt." Der freundliche aber bestimmte Herr in der blauen Uniform am Halleneingang weist jeden ab, der keine Eintrittskarte hat. Über zweitausend Zuhörer wollen Daniel Jonah Goldhagen, Autor des gefeier-

ten und verdammten Buches „Hitlers willige Vollstrecker – Ganz normale Deutsche“, sehen und hören.

Der Abend beginnt mit Musik. Musik von Ermordeten, geschrieben im Ghetto, im Vernichtungslager. Die vier Streicher verharren nach der letzten Note noch einen Augenblick mit den Geigenbögen in der Hand – so, als wollten sie den Ermordeten die letzte Ehre erweisen. Karl Bredthauer, Redaktionsmitglied der „Blätter für deutsche und internationale Politik“ und damit Vertreter des Demokratiepreisstifters, reicht den Musikern aus dem Blumenbukett vor dem Rednerpult eine rote Nelke.

Professor Jürgen Habermas, Inbegriff des kritischen Geistes auch zu Zeiten, als Nachdenklichkeit über deutsche Geschichte alles andere als en vogue war, hält die Laudatio auf Goldhagen. Er erinnert an die letzten Preisträger: Bärbel Bohley und Wolfgang Ullmann, stellvertretend für die Bürgerrechtler der DDR, und erklärt, warum nach nunmehr sieben Jahren der nicht regelmäßig verliehene Preis gerade an den jüdischen Amerikaner Goldhagen geht: „Er hat aufgrund der Eindringlichkeit und der moralischen Kraft seiner Darstellung dem öffentlichen Bewußtsein in der Bundesrepublik wesentliche Impulse gegeben, hat die Sensibilität für Hintergründe und Grenzen einer deutschen 'Normalisierung' geschärft.“

Gleich am Anfang nennt er eines der Grundprobleme deutscher historischer Forschung: „Seit den Anfängen der Bundesrepublik besteht ein Gesetz zwischen denen, die den Zivilisationsbruch lieber wie ein Naturereignis aus den Umständen erklären, und denen, die ihn eher verantwortlich handelnden Personen zuschreiben, und zwar nicht nur Hitler und seiner engsten Clique.“ Diese Fragestellung schließlich ist es ja, die zumindest einen Teil der großen Aufmerksamkeit erklärt, die Goldhagens Buch fand.

Jan Philipp Reemtsma, der gerade mit der Ausstellung seines Hamburger Instituts für Sozialforschung über Kriegsverbrechen der Wehrmacht erlebt, wie hart und unsachlich auch heute noch jemand kritisiert werden kann, der sicher geglaubte Erkenntnisse über die Vergangenheit mit sauber recherchierten Fakten zum Einsturz bringt, wendet sich in seinem Kommentar diesem Umstand zu: „Ein Bestseller ist ein Angebot, das eine bestehende Nachfrage befriedigt – worin bestand die?“

In seiner Antwort zieht er einen Bogen zu dem Film „Schindlers Liste“: „Nicht der endlich einmal gefundene ‘gute Deutsche’ war das, sondern das Thema der individuellen Verantwortung – anders gesagt, das der individuellen Freiheit.“ Menschen wollen heute nicht nur wissen, was geschichtlich passiert ist – sie wollen wissen, welche Motivationslagen zu welchen Handlungen geführt haben. Das ist nicht der einfache, aber der einzige Weg im Umgang mit Geschichte.

Die Erkenntnis, daß der Kreis derjenigen, die zur Mittäterschaft bereit waren, weit größer war als angenommen, bedeutet eben nicht, wie Goldhagens Kritiker gerne unterstellen, damit sei jeder Deutsche des Judenmords bezichtigt. Die Söhne und Töchter der Mörder, Mitläufer und Gegner der Nazis verlangen Aufklärung: „Als Bürger nehmen hingegen die Nachfahren ein öffentliches Interesse am dunkelsten Kapitel ihrer nationalen Geschichte im Hinblick auf sich selbst – und im Hinblick auf ihr Verhältnis zu den Opfern oder deren Nachkommen“ wahr. „Sie wollen sich über die kulturelle Matrix eines belastenden Erbes Klarheit verschaffen, um zu erkennen, wofür sie gemeinsam haften und was gegebenenfalls von den Traditionen, die damals einen verhängnisvollen Motivationshintergrund gebildet haben, noch fortwirkt und der Revision bedarf. Aus einem weit verbreiteten individuell schuldhaften Verhalten in der Vergangenheit entsteht das Bewußtsein kollektiver Haltung; mit der Zuschreibung kollektiver Schuld, die schon aus begrifflichen Gründen ein Unding ist, hat das nichts zu tun“, hält Habermas den Vereinfachern und Entstellern unter Goldhagens Kritikern entgegen.

Schmerzhaft ist die Arbeit des Amerikaners ja vor allem, weil ihre Ergebnisse einer weit verbreiteten Ansicht über den Mord an den Juden den Boden entziehen: „Hatte die Spaltung des Holocaust in zwei säuberlich voneinander geschiedene Vorgänge – das Töten in den Vernichtungslagern durch eine mörderische Elite und das Töten als scheinbar kriegsförmiger Akt, durch unterschiedlich uniformierte Einheiten exekutiert – dazu geführt, zunächst die historische Einmaligkeit der Vernichtungslager zu übersehen, dann nur noch diese in den Blick zu nehmen, so ist das Resultat ein bis heute nicht ausreichendes Verständnis der Gewaltdynamik selbst“, erklärt Reemtsma das Neue an Goldhagens Ansatz. Die „offen-

sichtliche Herzlosigkeit, die manchmal mit billiger Rührseligkeit kaschiert wird, die nur das auffälligste äußerliche Symptom einer tief verwurzelten, hartnäckigen und gelegentlich brutalen Weigerung" seien, „sich dem tatsächlich Geschehenen zu stellen und sich damit abzufinden", wie Hannah Arendt einmal schrieb, ist um so schwerer durchzuhalten, je weniger anonym und umstandsabhängig die Beweggründe und Täter selbst sind.

Liegen die Ursachen einmal bloß, kann der zweite Schritt getan werden: „Kann politische Massenkriminalität überhaupt einzelnen Personen oder Personengruppen zur Last gelegt werden", fragte Professor Jürgen Habermas sich und die gut zweitausend Zuhörer – und trennte dabei historisches Erkenntnisinteresse und strafrechtliche oder moralische Beurteilung. „Böse", so Habermas, „ist nicht die schiere Aggression als solche, sondern die, zu der sich der Täter berechtigt glaubt. Das Böse ist das verkehrte Gute. Daß viele Täter ihr mörderisches Handeln für legitim gehalten haben müssen, stützt Goldhagen mit vielen Details – vom fehlenden Bemühen um Geheimhaltung bis zu den obszönen Fototerminen." Wer sich mit Goldhagens Ergebnissen auseinandersetzt und die Forschungen anderer Wissenschaftler als Ergänzungen und nicht als Konkurrenz begreift, wird Geschichte als Chance zur Erkenntnis und nicht als Bedrohung oder zu verheimlichender Fehltritte begreifen.

„Wie lernt man aus der Geschichte?", fragt Goldhagen in seinem Dankwort. Denn das sei der Sinn auch seiner Arbeit gewesen: „Wer sich mit der Geschichte befaßt, kann aus ihr lernen und ist vermutlich weniger anfällig, deren dunkle Kapitel zu wiederholen. „Das demokratische Nachkriegsdeutschland sieht er dabei auf einem „beispielhaften Weg": „In der Bundesrepublik sind die Menschen mit einer genaueren Darstellung ihrer Geschichte konfrontiert, als Bürger anderer Länder es gewöhnt sind. Ich kenne kein anderes Land, das so offen und konsequent mit den unrühmlichen und schrecklichen Kapiteln der eigenen Vergangenheit umgeht", sagt der Mann, dem so oft vorgeworfen wird, er wolle ein ganzes Volk zu Massenmördern stempeln. Den Grund für den beispielhaften Umgang der Deutschen mit ihrer Geschichte sieht Goldhagen in der „Internationalisierung" der deutschen Geschichtswissen-

schaft: „Externe Sichtweisen korrigieren zumindest zum Teil zwei der größten Fehler des Nationalstaates: zum einen seine Tendenz zur Selbstverherrlichung, wobei viel von der Nationalgeschichte abhängt; zum anderen den Drang, dem zu folgen, was er als die eigenen Interessen begreift, auch wenn den anderen daraus erhebliche Nachteile erwachsen.

Demokratie und „internationalistische Geschichtsschreibung" hängen für Goldhagen eng zusammen und sind große Vorzüge Nachkriegs(west)deutschlands: „Zwei parallel verlaufende, überraschende Entwicklungen kennzeichnen die Bundesrepublik: Das eine ist die Herausbildung einer relativ nicht-nationalistischen und bemerkenswert selbstkritischen Nationalgeschichte, das andere die Entstehung eines relativ nicht-nationalistischen, international verantwortungsvoll agierenden Nationalstaates" – das „Modell Deutschland", so lautet der Titel von Goldhagens Vorwort. Dabei glaubt er nicht, daß diese positive Entwicklung allein dem Einfluß der Westmächte zu danken sei, vielmehr ist ein Zusammenwirken demokratischer Deutscher mit demokratischen Ausländern und die Einsicht in eine gemeinsame Interessenlage Grund für die Entwicklung gewesen. Denen, die glauben, ein international zurückhaltend und geschichtlich bewußtes Deutschland würde sich vor anderen lächerlich machen, hält Goldhagen entgegen: „Sie liegen falsch. Exakt das Gegenteil ist der Fall. Das politische Verhalten der Bundesrepublik sollte Anlaß zur Genugtuung geben. Ihre Art, Politik zu machen, ist ein festes Merkmal der deutschen Demokratie, eine unleugbare Stärke des Landes. Deshalb sollte sich nicht die Bundesrepublik, sondern sollten sich andere Länder wandeln. Es ist an der Zeit, dieses deutsche Modell zu internationalisieren", verlangt er Lernfähigkeit von den einstigen Lehrern.

Starker Tobak für die Bewohner des Landes, die sich über Bundesregierung und Geschichtsblindheit erregen, nicht länger hinnehmen wollen, daß die Opfer der mörderischen Hitleranhänger verleumdet und verarmt sterben, nie eine Entschädigung sehen oder von Behörde zu Behörde verwiesen werden, während die Täter „Opferrenten" beziehen und eine Verurteilung vor Gericht kaum zu befürchten haben. Vielleicht ist es die Nähe zu den Dingen, das tägliche Ausgesetzt-Sein, was uns den Blick verstellt, der sich jemandem, der von der anderen Seite des Atlantiks

kommt, eröffnet. Daß keineswegs alles zum besten steht, ist Goldhagen natürlich klar: „Die Proteste der letzten Zeit gegen die Wehrmachtsausstellung machen deutlich, daß noch immer Widerstand gegen grundlegende Wahrheiten geleistet wird", konstatiert der Amerikaner.

Er selber sieht sich auf den Schultern derer stehen, die vor ihm gearbeitet haben: „Daß ich in Deutschland für ein Buch mit solch verunsicherndem und schmerzvollem Inhalt ausgezeichnet werde, ist der eindrucksvollste Beleg für alles, was ich heute abend gesagt habe, für Charakter und Versprechungen des heutigen Deutschland, und für die Tatsache, daß vielmehr diejenigen, die die von mir hier charakterisierte Bundesrepublik möglich gemacht haben und ihre Grundprinzipien verfechten, diesen Preis verdient haben." Während Goldhagen dies sagt, steht vor der Beethoven-Halle ein Dutzend derer, die nicht zuhören wollen: „Wir wollten mit einigen Freunden hier einen sichtbaren Protest anbringen, damit Goldhagen nicht in Amerika erzählen kann, alle Deutschen hätten ihm die Füße geküßt für seine Lügen."

Jochen Börst, in: „Neues Deutschland", 12.3.1997

Deutschland als Modell

In lauer Abendluft standen einige versprengte Unbelehrbare vor der Bonner Beethovenhalle und beschimpften die Preisverleiher auf Handzetteln als „Goldhagens willige Vollstrecker". Die unerwartet zahlreich herbeiströmenden Gäste nahmen davon keine Notiz. Die Polizei hatte es freilich für nötig befunden, zum Schutz der Veranstaltung mit einigen Mannschaftswagen vorzufahren. Erwies sich diese Maßnahme auch als überflüssig, so wurde doch im Saal selbst zur Genüge deutlich, daß Daniel Goldhagen und sein Buch über „Hitlers willige Vollstrecker" auch im demokratischen Lager immer noch polarisieren.

Jan Philipp Reemtsma. *Foto: Josef Menzen*

Während liberale und linksliberale Politprominenz in beachtlicher Stärke – von Antje Vollmer über Hans-Ulrich Klose bis zu Joschka Fischer – erschienen war, glänzten zumindest die höheren Chargen der Regierungsseite durch Abwesenheit. Niemand hatte erwartet, daß Peter Gauweiler dem US-Politologen seine Aufwartung machte; aber daß andere, aufgeschlossenere Vertreter im Auditorium fehlten – das war beschämend.

Als wenn Goldhagen, dem Karlheinz Koppe den mit 10 000 Mark dotierten „Demokratiepreis" der „Blätter für deutsche und internationale Politik" überreichte, das rechtsradikale Gerede von seinem angeblichen „Deutschenhaß" gezielt Lügen strafen wollte, stellte er seine Dankesrede unter das Motto „Modell Deutschland". Er kenne kein Land, führte er mit liebenswert amerikanischem Akzent aus, „das so offen und konsequent mit den unrühmlichen und schrecklichen Kapiteln seiner eigenen Vergangenheit umgeht".

Leute, die einer Schlußstrichmentalität frönten, „liegen falsch", denn gerade die offensive und pluralistische – das heißt die internationale Diskussion einbeziehende – Auseinandersetzung mit der eigenen Nationalgeschichte beweise die Stärke der deutschen Demokratie und zeige, daß die Mentalitäten der Vergangenheit überwunden seien. Dieses Loblied hielt Goldhagen freilich nicht davon ab, „angemessene Anerkennung und

Entschädigung“ für Opfer des Holocaust wie Homosexuelle sowie Sinti und Roma zu fordern.

Vorangegangen waren die Laudationes von Jürgen Habermas und Jan Philipp Reemtsma. Es spricht für Habermas, daß er an keiner Stelle einem dunstigen Enthusiasmus für den Geehrten verfiel, sondern sich seines Themas aus der Distanz zu versichern suchte – was freundlich formulierte Kritik einschloß. Auf diese Weise gelang es ihm, Goldhagen genau so wie seinen – seriösen Widersachern gerecht zu werden, ohne daß das Ganze nach einem krampfigen Spagat aussah.

Nationales Projekt?

Vorbehalte machte der Frankfurter Sozialphilosoph gegen Goldhagens Qualifizierung des Holocaust als eines „nationalen Projekts der Deutschen“ geltend: „Gegen diesen Goldhagen, der den Kredit seiner empirischen Untersuchungen intentionalistisch zu überziehen und daraus einen globalen Geltungsanspruch abzuleiten scheint, kann man Goldhagen selbst ins Feld führen – den, der sich entschieden gegen monokausale Ansätze wehrt, der sich für ein komparatives Vorgehen stark macht und natürlich weiß, daß man sich für die Erklärung des Holocaust „nicht allein auf den Antisemitismus beschränken“ kann.“

Ein Schwerpunkt von Habermas' Ausführungen war die durch das Buch und seine Rezeption in Deutschland nahegelegte Frage nach dem richtigen „öffentlichen Gebrauch der Historie“. Dabei wandte er sich gegen diejenigen, die Goldhagens Arbeit unterstellen, das heutige Deutschland diskreditieren und zukunftsunfähig machen zu wollen. Die „erklärenden Zurechnungen“ des Historikers – wer war für welche Verbrechen verantwortlich? – hätten, sobald sie in die Diskussion von Nachgeborenen über ihr politisches Zusammenleben einbezogen würden, keine moralisierende Funktion.

Es gehe dabei also nicht um die Zuschreibung von „Kollektivschuld“, sondern darum, „sich über die kulturelle Matrix eines belastenden Erbes Klarheit zu verschaffen, um zu erkennen, wofür sie gemeinsam haften und was gebenenfalls von den Traditionen, die damals einen verhängnis-

vollen Motivationshintergrund gebildet haben, noch fortwirkt und der Revision bedarf. Diesen Diskurs beflügelt zu haben, sei das Verdienst des Preisträgers.

Reemtsma stellte das Goldhagen-Buch in eine Linie mit den Tagebüchern von Viktor Klemperer und der Wehrmacht-Ausstellung seines Hamburger Instituts für Sozialforschung und begründete den Erfolg dieser drei „Ereignisse" mit einem Bruch etablierter Traditionen der Historiographie. Während die Geschichtsschreibung von Haus aus dazu neige, darzustellen, daß alles habe so kommen müssen, wie es gekommen sei, machten Goldhagen, Klemperer und die Ausstellung Handlungsspielräume sichtbar, rückten die individuelle Freiheit und Verantwortung eines jeden Handelnden ins Bewußtsein.

Beim Publikum sei „die Furcht vor der Betrachtung des Jedermann und der Möglichkeit, in ihm den eigenen Großvater, Vater oder Onkel wiederzuerkennen, durch die Bereitschaft ersetzt worden, sich diesem Erkenntnisrisiko auszusetzen". Goldhagens Buch habe „einen nicht mehr wegzudenkenden Beitrag zu jener Diskussion des historischen Faktenmaterials geliefert, die allein in der Lage ist, den von Hannah Arendt bei ihrem Deutschlandbesuch 1950 konstatierten „allgemeinen Gefühlsmangel" und jene „offensichtliche Herzlosigkeit, die manchmal mit billiger Rührseligkeit kaschiert wird", zu überwinden".

Markus Schwering, in: „Kölner Stadtanzeiger", 12.3.1997

Diskursethischer Segen

Mit dem durch Ernst Nolte ausgelösten Historikerstreit wurden auf seiten der Linken schlafende Hunde geweckt. Seit Mitte der siebziger Jahre war von ihr der Paradigmenwechsel von der Gesellschaftstheorie zur Beschäftigung mit Geschichte verschlafen worden. Zuvor schon hatte

Michael Stürmer seinem Kanzler erklärt, daß die Eroberung der Zukunft auch vom Interpretationsmonopol über die Geschichte abhängig sei...

„Geschichtswissenschaft degeneriert zu Geschichtspolitik", so Jürgen Habermas, „sobald die Sicht des analysierenden Beobachters mit der Perspektive verschmilzt, die die Teilnehmer an Selbstverständigungsdiskursen einnehmen." Doch sowohl die Laudatio des Sozialphilosophen als auch die Begründung der preisstiftenden Monatsschrift *Blätter für deutsche und internationale Politik* ließen keinen Zweifel, daß es sich bei der Demokratiepreis-Verleihung 1997 an Daniel Goldhagen um ein geschichtspolitisch gewolltes Ereignis handelt.

Der Anlaß scheint konstruiert, die Begründung nicht sehr schlüssig. Ihm sei „umgekehrter Rassismus", eine Neuauflage der „Kollektivschuld"-These und der Nachweis „genetisch bedingter Mordgelüste der Deutschen" unterstellt worden. Wer den Historikerstreit am Ende der Achtziger noch als rechthaberisch verbiesterte Seniorenveranstaltung in Erinnerung hat, scheint dem sympathischen Medienstar Goldhagen manche Ungereimtheit nachzusehen. So widerspricht denn auch Habermas mit Recht dem falschen Eindruck der Preisbegründung.

Ebenso fragwürdig ist sicher auch die Begründung, Goldhagens zusätzlicher Anerkennungsapplaus für die Bonner Demokratie sei beim deutschen Publikum nicht so recht angekommen. Das Lob „laufe ins Leere". Dies nur deutscher Borniertheit anzulasten, scheint ein wenig vermessen. Während die Begründung überdies Goldhagens „moralische Kraft seiner Darstellung" preist, merkt Jürgen Habermas an: „Hier geht es nicht primär um Schuld oder Entschuldung der Vorfahren, sondern um eine kritische Selbstvergewisserung der Nachkommen."

Die Goldhagen-Studie empfängt den diskursethischen Segen: Aus einem weit verbreiteten individuell schuldhaften Verhalten in der Vergangenheit, wie es am abscheulichen Beispiel mörderischer Polizeibataillone gezeigt wird, entstehe das Bewußtsein kollektiver Haftung: „Mit der Zuschreibung kollektiver Schuld (...) hat das nichts zu tun." Habermas hält es für zwingend, daß derartige Verbrechen, wie sie Goldhagen auch im Kapitel über die „Todesmärsche" beschreibt, ohne „starke normative Gründe" nicht denkbar sind. Deshalb rekurriere die Studie naheliegen-

derweise auf Vorstellungen von „dem Juden". Nach Habermas liefert Goldhagen damit ein begrüßenswertes Exempel für die Erschütterung eines „naiven Vertrauensvorschusses von eigenen Traditionen", mit denen konservative Geister noch immer die „Zukunftsfähigkeit" des eigenen Volkes beschwören möchten.

In seinem „Kommentar" zur Preisverleihung ging Jan Philip Reemtsma noch einen Schritt weiter. Mit der ebenso zutreffenden wie verschleiernden Begrifflichkeit von der „industriellen Vernichtung" sei über Jahrzehnte der Blick auf die Täterperspektive verstellt worden. Die „Furcht vor der Betrachtung eines Jedermann" habe nur die Scheinalternative zwischen Mittäterschaft oder selbstmörderischem Widerstand zugelassen. Noch „Schindlers Liste" ist vielerorts als willkommenes Exkulpationsangebot vom guten Deutschen mißverstanden worden. Das Thema des Films sei aber in Wahrheit die individuelle Verantwortung. Reemtsma schlägt einen paradigmatischen Bogen von den Tagebüchern Victor Klemperers über die Wehrmachtsausstellung seines Hamburger Instituts bis zu Goldhagens *Hitlers willige Vollstrecker*. Gegen das Töten als „scheinbar kriegsförmiger Akt" steht die plausible Vermutung, man habe auch anders handeln können.

Den Protagonisten der gut organisierten Veranstaltung erscheint Goldhagens Oeuvre als Mahnmal gegen die drohende Desensibilisierung eines normalisierten Deutschland. Von den potentiellen Gefahren beim Übergang zur Berliner Republik handelte denn auch die Dankesrede des glücklichen Preisträgers.

Norbert Seitz, in: „Süddeutsche Zeitung", 12.3.1997

„Man muß die Deutschen loben"

taz: Was war das beeindruckendste Erlebnis für Sie nach Erscheinen Ihres Buches „Hitlers willige Vollstrecker"?

Daniel Goldhagen: Viele gute Dinge sind passiert. Nach einem Vortrag sagte mir ein alter jüdischer Mann: „Auf dieses Buch habe ich 50 Jahre gewartet.“ Später sagte mir eine junge Deutsche: „Ich möchte, daß Sie wissen, daß Sie meiner Nation einen großen Dienst erwiesen haben.“

Im vergangenen Jahr haben Sie die Deutschen mit „Hitlers willige Vollstrecker“ vor den Kopf gestoßen. Nun loben Sie ihre beispielhafte demokratische Entwicklung. Verfolgen Sie damit eine pädagogische Absicht – nach dem Prinzip Zuckerbrot und Peitsche?

Ich habe in meinem Buch versucht, mit wissenschaftlicher Genauigkeit den Holocaust, vor allem die Motive der Täter, zu analysieren. Viele Leute stecken mich nun in eine Schublade. Sie erwarten von mir, daß ich das, was im Buch steht, auf die heutige Bundesrepublik übertrage. Dabei ist doch offensichtlich, daß sich hier eine echte Demokratie entwickelt hat. Das ist kein Widerspruch zu dem, was ich über die Vergangenheit geschrieben habe. Vielmehr war das richtige Verständnis der Geschichte das zentrale Moment für die Entwicklung der Bundesrepublik. Die Deutschen haben aus ihrer Geschichte gelernt. Ein Hitler, der heute von der Rolle des Blutes in der Menschheitsgeschichte schwadronierte, würde für verrückt erklärt.

Ist es nicht selbstverständlich, daß gerade die Deutschen sich mit ihrer Vergangenheit intensiver auseinandersetzen als andere?

Die Japaner haben während des Zweiten Weltkrieges ähnliche Verbrechen begangen wie die Deutschen. Japan hat seine Vergangenheit aber nicht annähernd so aufgearbeitet. Die Demokratie kam in Deutschland auch nicht plötzlich. Das war ein schwieriger Prozeß. Von zentraler Bedeutung war die 68er-Bewegung, die bewußte Auseinandersetzung der Kinder mit ihren Eltern und deren Vergangenheit. 1965 hatten viele noch kein rechtes Vertrauen in die Dauerhaftigkeit der deutschen Demokratie. Mitte der 80er hat sich das völlig geändert. Die Geschichte der Bundesrepublik ist die größte Erfolgsstory der Nachkriegszeit. Sie zeigt, daß sich Gesellschaften neu erschaffen können.

Hat es mit der Mentalität der Deutschen zu tun, daß sich die Bundesrepublik zu einer, wie Sie sagen, vorbildlichen Demokratie entwickeln konnte?

Was ist Mentalität? Solche Kategorien verwende ich nicht. Es gibt nicht den charakteristischen Deutschen. Die Deutschen haben nach Hit-

ler auch nicht einfach auf Demokratie umgeschaltet, weil es von außen jemand gesagt hat und sie folgsam genug waren. Entscheidend für die Demokratisierung war, was ich Internationalisierung nenne. Druck von außen, direkte Beteiligung Außenstehender haben zur Integration kritischer Perspektiven in die deutsche Nationalgeschichte geführt.

Ist dies ein Modell für fundamentale gesellschaftliche Veränderungen?

Ja, schauen Sie sich den amerikanischen Süden an. Noch 1960 unterstützte die große Mehrheit der Weißen die gesetzliche Rassentrennung. Und schon Anfang der 80er war sie dagegen. Was ist passiert? Es gab enormen Druck von außen, vom Norden, von Washington. Natürlich ist noch nicht alles wunderbar. Aber im Laufe einer Generation haben sich nicht nur Institutionen, sondern auch Einstellungen ändern lassen.

Geht die demokratische Entwicklung Deutschlands auch mit einem Rückgang von Antisemitismus und Fremdenfeindlichkeit einher?

Antisemitismus gibt es immer noch, aber er hat an Intensität verloren und ist weniger virulent. Niemand würde mehr auf die Idee kommen, Juden als Teufel in Menschengestalt zu bezeichnen. Natürlich gibt es auch noch Fremdenfeindlichkeit, etwa gegenüber Türken und anderen Minderheiten. Aber im großen und ganzen sind Juden und Ausländer Teil der deutschen Gesellschaft geworden. Jedenfalls habe ich keinerlei Befürchtungen, daß es in Deutschland zu einer antisemitischen Explosion kommen könnte. Was systematische Gewalt gegen Minderheiten angeht, ist Deutschland sicher eines der letzten Länder, an die wir dabei denken.

Schließen Sie in Ihr Lob Ostdeutschland mit ein?

Natürlich ist die Geschichte der DDR ganz anders verlaufen als in der Bundesrepublik. Nach dem Fall der Mauer war ein Lernprozeß erforderlich. Es war nicht einfach, so wie es in Westdeutschland in den 50ern nicht einfach war. Aber ich bin zuversichtlich, daß in der nächsten Generation die demokratische Orientierung sich nicht mehr von der in Westdeutschland unterscheiden wird.

Worin bestehen die Unterschiede genau?

Da muß ich passen. Ich habe den Prozeß in Ostdeutschland nicht genau genug verfolgt.

Und wie beurteilen Sie die Entwicklung Österreichs?

Oh, welche Länder wollen wir heute noch durchgehen? (lacht) Österreich hat eine demokratische Gesellschaft aufgebaut. Aber in Österreich hat es nicht diese Internationalisierung wie in Deutschland gegeben. Warum? Das mag an dem Mythos gelegen haben, daß die Österreicher die ersten Opfer des Nazismus waren. Weil sie nicht in derselben Weise wie die Deutschen verantwortlich für den Holocaust gemacht wurden, waren sie auch nicht dem gleichen internationalen Druck ausgesetzt.

In Ihrer Rede anläßlich der Verleihung des Demokratiepreises der „Blätter für deutsche und internationale Politik" empfehlen Sie anderen Ländern die Bundesrepublik als Vorbild. Was ist Ihre Botschaft an Deutschland?

Daß die Diskussion, die sich um mein Buch und auch um die Wehrmachtsausstellung entsponnen hat, eine gute Sache ist. Und daß es weiterhin einen kontinuierlichen Prozeß des Verstehens und der Diskussion über die Vergangenheit geben sollte.

Das klingt so unspektakulär, nach dem Trubel, den Sie mit Ihrem Buch verursacht haben.

Wie oft haben Sie das schon gehört, daß jemand die Deutschen für ihre demokratische Entwicklung so gelobt hat? Dieser Erfolg der Deutschen hat bisher nicht genügend Erwähnung gefunden. Natürlich besteht dabei immer die Gefahr, daß die Leute auf Lob selbstgefällig reagieren. Aber man muß die Wahrheit sagen. Ich hoffe, es wird für die Leute glaubwürdiger, das Lob zu akzeptieren, wenn es ausgerechnet von mir kommt.

Interview: Markus Franz, Damian Müller, in: „die tageszeitung", 13.3.1997

Ein Lob, das ratlos machte

Ein derartiges Kompliment hatte an diesem Abend wohl niemand erwartet. Schon gar nicht vom Autor des Bestsellers „Hitlers willige Vollstrecker". Erstaunlich selbstkritisch, lobte Daniel Jonah Goldhagen, sei-

en die Deutschen im Umgang mit ihrer Vergangenheit. Die meisten der zweitausend Zuschauer, die bei der Verleihung des Demokratiepreises der „Blätter für deutsche und internationale Politik" in Bonn dabeisein wollten, mußte dieses Lob ratlos machen. Hatten sie nicht vorher in Jürgen Habermas' Laudatio gehört, daß Goldhagen das notwendige Gegenstück zu einer konservativen Geschichtsverharm-losung geschrieben habe? Hatte ihnen nicht Jan-Philipp Reemtsma in seiner Rede erklärt, daß die kollektive Bereitschaft, sich der Vergangenheit zu stellen, erst mit Goldhagens Buch, der Wehrmachts-Ausstellung und den Klemperer-Tagebüchern „unerwartete Erfolge" aufzuweisen habe?

Für die Kritik am deutschen Umgang mit der Vergangenheit gab es Beifall, bei Goldhagens Lob auf ebendiesen Umgang malte sich eher verlegene Ratlosigkeit auf den Gesichtern ab. Und gerade deshalb liegt der Verdacht nahe, daß viele nicht nur gekommen waren, um den Preisträger zu ehren, sondern auch, um sich selbst als aufrechte Minderheit inmitten der geschichtsvergessenen Mehrheit zu feiern. Den Thesen von den „willigen Vollstreckern" zuzustimmen heißt für sie, Widerstand gegen einen neokonservativen Zeitgeist zu leisten. Goldhagens Dankesrede ließ – möglicherweise unbeabsichtigt – diese Haltung als einen Widerstand erscheinen, der nichts kostet, weil die berechtigte Forderung nach einem schuldbewußten und schuldzuweisenden Blick auf die deutsche Geschichte längst in der wissenschaftlichen und öffentlichen Diskussion eingelöst wurde.

Reemtsma, Goldhagen und Habermas vor der Preisverleihung. Foto: dpa

Als der Demokratie-Preisträger nach seinem Lob für die deutsche Aufarbeitung der Vergangenheit dazu ermahnte, sich für eine angemessene Anerkennung der nichtjüdischen Opfer der nationalsozialistischen Vernichtungspolitik einzusetzen, war im Publikum fast so etwas wie Erleichterung ob der neuen Herausforderung zu spüren – eine Reaktion, so zwiespältig wie der ganze Abend.

Christiane Florin, in: „Rheinischer Merkur", 14.3.1997

Gipfeltreffen

Ein intellektuelles Ereignis, ein kleines Gipfeltreffen eigener Art: Das war wohl der Grund für das gewaltige Interesse an einem Abend mit Jürgen Habermas (rechts), Jan Philipp Reemtsma (links) und Daniel J. Goldhagen (Mitte) diese Woche in Bonn. *Die Blätter für deutsche und internationale Politik*, ein Forum für aktuelle und grundsätzliche Streitfragen, hatten dem jungen amerikanischen Historiker den „Demokratiepreis 1997" für sein Buch über"Hitlers willige Vollstrecker" verliehen. Die Blätter, deren Herausgebergremium von Günter Gaus bis Walter Jens, von Rudolf Hickel bis Claus Leggewie, von Jens Reich bis Rosemarie Will für eine große Bandbreite zeitgenössischen Denkens bürgt, hatten Habermas und Reemtsma als Laudatoren eingeladen.

Habermas hatte sich zu Goldhagens Thesen bisher nicht geäußert. Viele der intellektuellen Weggefährten des Sozialphilosophen unter den Historikern waren aus fachlicher Sicht auf Distanz zu Goldhagen und seiner Ansicht gegangen, im Genozid hätten „die Deutschen" ihren tiefverwurzelten Antisemitismus nur vollstreckt. Gerade namhafte NS-Forscher, die sich allen Normalisierungsabsichten querstellten, sahen sich plötzlich in der Defensive. Allein deshalb war man gerade auf die Laudatio von Habermas, die wir hier veröffentlichen, besonders gespannt. In

seiner Dankesrede wollte Goldhagen nachweisen, daß vor allem die „Internationalisierung" der Nationalgeschichte zu einer bemerkenswerten historischen Ehrlichkeit in Deutschland geführt habe. Es sei an der Zeit, dieses „deutsche Modell" zu internationalisieren. Fast unfreiwillig ging Goldhagen dabei über die Laudatoren hinaus und beförderte sich selbst zum Kronzeugen für eine Entwicklung der Bundesrepublik in die richtige Richtung. Vielleicht war es dieser Zungenschlag, der dazu führte, daß man den Abend doch auch mit gemischten Gefühlen verließ.

Gunter Hofmann, in: „Die Zeit", 14.3.1997

Gründlich gelernt

Ein verschwiegenes Jubiläum: Vor zehn Jahren verliehen die *Blätter für deutsche und internationale Politik*, damals – vor allem materiell – noch stärker orientiert an den Werten des Ostens, erstmalig ihren „Demokratiepreis". In seiner Einleitungsrede zur Preisverleihung 1987 erläuterte einer der Blätter-Begründer, Paul B. Neuhöffer, wozu dieser Preis gut sein sollte. Die „Leitmotive der Bonner Republik", Demokratie und Frieden, seien „schon im Gründungsakt und in den folgenden Jahrzehnten verletzt, unterhöhlt und umgebogen" worden. Allerdings gebe es auch „ein ständiges und in den letzten Jahren der Friedensbewegung und der zahlreichen sozialen Bewegungen stark anwachsendes Gegengewicht gegen den demokratieverkürzenden Konsens der „freiheitlich-demokratischen Grundordnung", einer auf die sogenannte atlantische Wertegemeinschaft geschrumpften Demokratie-Auffassung". Diese Gegenkraft wollte die 1955 gegründete wissenschaftliche Monatszeitschrift stärken. Das Auditorium, zu dem unter anderem der sowjetische Botschafter in Bonn, ein stellvertretender Minister für Kultur der DDR und eine Vertreterin des

ANC gehörten, vernahm es zustimmend. Den Preis erhielt damals die „Arbeitsgruppe Alternative Wirtschaftspolitik".

Zeiten und Auditorien ändern sich, der „Demokratiepreis" ist geblieben. Heute setzen sich die Blätter für „eine über bündnispolitische und ökonomische Bindungen hinausgehende Westorientierung des Landes" ein, und die Geschichte des „Demokratiepreises" fängt inzwischen anders an: mit der Preisverleihung an die „Demokratiebewegung der DDR", vertreten durch Bärbel Bohley und Wolfgang Ullmann, im Jahre 1990. Zur diesjährigen Preisverleihung am vergangenen Montag in der gefüllten Bonner Beethovenhalle kamen zwar keine Vertreter der UdSSR und der DDR mehr, dafür aber aller im Bundestag vertretenen Parteien, angeführt von den Bundestagspräsidiumsmitgliedern Hans-Ulrich Klose und Antje Vollmer. Verliehen wurde der „Demokratiepreis 1997" an Daniel Jonah Goldhagen, da er „dem öffentlichen Bewußtsein in der Bundesrepublik Deutschland wesentliche Impulse gegeben" habe, und zwar „in einer den Übergang von der Bonner zur Berliner Republik prägenden Zeit". Als Laudatioren für Goldhagen waren Jürgen Habermas und Jan Philipp Reemtsma geladen.

Ein Neubelebung der Goldhagen-Debatte beabsichtigten die Blätter allerdings mit ihrer Entscheidung nicht. Bisher sei die Anerkennung, die Goldhagen „der Bundesrepublik als einem neuen, in der politischen Zivilisation der Moderne, im Westen endlich (halbwegs) angekommenen Deutschland zollt", so Blätter-Redakteur Karl D. Bredthauer, weitgehend ignoriert worden. Hier gebe es „zwischen deutschen Kritikern und deutschen Befürwortern Daniel Goldhagens (...) eine merkwürdige Übereinstimmung". Mit diesem Mißverständnis hat Goldhagen nun unüberhörbar aufgeräumt. Denn in seiner unter dem Motto „Modell Deutschland" stehenden Dankesrede, konzentrierte er sich diesmal nicht auf Hitlers willige Vollstrecker, sondern auf Deutschlands willige Demokraten, die mit Hilfe des Westens richtigen Schlüsse aus einem „nationalen Trauma" gezogen hätten: „Es ist Zeit, daß andere Nationen der Bundesrepublik in Sachen Nationalgeschichtsschreibung und Selbstverständnis nacheifern."

Die *FAZ* brachte die Sichtweise Goldhagens präzise auf den Punkt: „Nach dem Inferno, das die ganz gewöhnlichen Deutschen angerichtet

haben, haben sie jetzt, genauso gewöhnlich wie damals, nur ungewöhnlich gut belehrt durch ihre Freunde, das Paradies der exportfähigen Demokratie erreicht. Das 'Modell Deutschland' hat Serienreife erlangt". Eine Botschaft, die jedoch überhaupt nicht in ihr Goldhagen-Bild paßt. Daher beschäftigte sich die FAZ auch in ihrem Bericht über die Preisverleihung nicht weiter mit dem Inhalt seiner Rede, sondern kolportierte stattdessen lieber noch einmal alle Diffamierungen der „historischen Fachwelt" gegen Goldhagen. Der Süddeutschen Zeitung zufolge handelte die Dankesrede von „den potentiellen Gefahren beim Übergang zur Berliner Republik". Der SZ-Redakteur muß auf einer anderen Veranstaltung gewesen sein. Denn so gut ist Deutschland schon lange nicht mehr weggekommen.

„Das politische Verhalten der Bundesrepublik sollte Anlaß zur Genugtuung geben", meint Goldhagen: „Ihre Art, Politik zu machen, ist ein festes Merkmal der deutschen Demokratie, eine unleugbare Stärke des Landes." Dies sollten „Deutsche und Nichtdeutsche ... gleichermaßen verstehen, begrüßen, ermutigen und fördern". Auch kenne er „kein anderes Land, das so offen und konsequent mit den unrühmlichen und schrecklichen Kapiteln der eigenen Vergangenheit umgeht". Die Deutschen hätten gründlich aus ihrer Geschichte gelernt, so der Preisträger. Das zeige sich etwa daran, so erläuterte er der taz, daß „ein Hitler, der heute von der Rolle des Blutes in der Menschheitsgeschichte schwadronierte, ... für verrückt erklärt" würde. Ein Hitler schwadroniert zwar nicht mehr in Deutschland über die „Rolle des Blutes", doch für den Erwerb der deutschen Staatsbürgerschaft gilt grundsätzlich immer noch das jus sanguinis. Diejenigen, die für dessen Beibehaltung sorgen, werden leider in keiner Weise für verrückt erklärt.

So scharfsinnig, wie er sich mit der deutschen Vergangenheit vor 1945 auseinandergesetzt hat, so erschreckend oberflächlich bleibt seine Betrachtung der deutschen Nachkriegsentwicklung und Gegenwart. Jan Philipp Reemtsmas brillante Laudatio auf Goldhagen läßt sich als Gegenrede lesen, wenn er die „spezifisch deutsche Verleugnisdynamik" analysiert und feststellt, Goldhagen habe mit seinem Buch einen „nicht mehr wegzudenkenden Beitrag zu jener Diskussion des historischen Fakten-

materials geleistet, die allein (...) in der Lage ist, den von Hannah Arendt bei ihrem Deutschlandbesuch 1950 konstatierten 'allgemeine(n) Gefühlsmangel', und jene 'offensichtliche Herzlosigkeit, die manchmal mit billiger Rührseligkeit kaschiert wird', zu überwinden, 'die nur das auffälligste äußerliche Symptom einer tief verwurzelten, hartnäckigen und gelegentlich brutalen Weigerung' seien, 'sich dem tatsächlich Geschehenen zu stellen und sich damit abzufinden".

Wenn Goldhagen von der hervorragenden Entwicklung Deutschlands nach 1945 spricht, meint er selbstverständlich nur den Westteil. In seiner Bonner Rede fand die DDR nur einmal indirekte Erwähnung: „Dem Westteil Deutschlands blieb anfangs keine andere Wahl, als die demokratischen Institutionen zu übernehmen. Viele übernahmen sie gern – nicht nur, weil sie die Demokratie für etwas Wünschenswertes hielten, die Bedrohung durch den kommunistischen Osten machte das westliche Lager zur einzig attraktiven Wahl."

Sein Bild von der DDR ist zwar, wie er gegenüber der *taz* zugab, von Unkenntnis geprägt, „da er den Prozeß in Ostdeutschland nicht genau genug verfolgt habe", und trotzdem steht sein Urteil fest: „Natürlich ist die Geschichte der DDR ganz anders verlaufen als in der Bundesrepublik. Nach dem Fall der Mauer war ein Lernprozeß erforderlich. Es war nicht einfach, so wie es in Westdeutschland in den fünfziger Jahren nicht einfach war." Kaum verwunderlich, daß bei einer solchen Betrachtungsweise die Kontinuität des Antikommunismus ausgeblendet bleibt, der es den willigen Helfern Nazi-Deutschlands so einfach machte, bruchlos in der Bundesrepublik ihre Karrieren fortzusetzen.

Goldhagen hält die Geschichte der Bundesrepublik für „die Erfolgsstory der Nachkriegszeit". Damit hat er vollständig recht. Es ist beeindruckend, wie aus Besiegten letztlich doch Sieger werden konnten. Das war jedoch nur möglich, indem es eben nicht die von ihm konstatierte „Ehrlichkeit im Umgang mit der Vergangenheit" gab, sondern das Prinzip des „kommunikativen Beschweigens" der individuellen Verantwortung und das Verstecken hinter Institutionen und Strukturen.

Um Goldhagen nicht unrecht zu tun: Seine Lobpreisung der „außerordentlichen Errungenschaften der Bundesrepublik" dürfen nicht

mißverstanden werden. Er ist nicht der Ansicht daß nun ein „Schlußstrich“ unter die deutsche Vergangenheit gezogen werden könnte. Im Gegenteil: Er fordert, daß sie in den Köpfen leben dig gehalten wird, um eine sonst drohende Wiederholung zu verhindern. Daniel Goldhagen ist ein antifaschistischer Liberaler – und bleibt daher ein Haßobjekt für die Geschichts-Entsorger-Fraktion, die immer noch größer ist, als Goldhagen wahrhaben will. Wer allerdings in Goldhagen einen Kronzeugen gegen das wiedererstarkte Deutschland sehen wollte, dürfte spätestens seit letzter Woche kuriert sein.

Pascal Beucker, in: „junge Welt“, 15./16.3.1997

Schwierigkeiten mit der Normalität

Nun haben das umstrittene Buch und die verstörte Debatte, die es ausgelöst hat, sozusagen ihren Platz gefunden. So etwa wird man die Verleihung des Demokratie-Preises an den amerikanischen Historiker Daniel J. Goldhagen in der vergangenen Woche in Bonn wohl verstehen dürfen. Aber weder die Fragwürdigkeit seiner Grundthese, im Mord an den Juden hätten die Deutschen nur ihre beispiellose antisemitische Verderbtheit ausgelebt, noch die Mängel, die die Historiker seinem Buch bescheinigten, haben dabei eine Rolle gespielt. Es ist die Wirkung auf die Öffentlichkeit, die als der zu preisende Ertrag der stürmischen Wochen im Herbst übrig geblieben ist. Goldhagen habe, so hieß es in der Begründung der Preisverleihung, die „Sensibilität für Hintergründe und Grenzen einer deutschen ‚Normalisierung‘ geschärft“.

Den jungen amerikanischen Historiker, der übrigens in seiner Dankesrede seine deutschen Kollegen gar nicht genug loben konnte, gar ein „deutsches Modell“ der Vergangenheitsbewältigung ausmachte, kann man für diese nationalpädagogische Wendung nicht in Anspruch nehmen. Sie ist genuin deutscher Herkunft – was man schon an der feinen

Distanzierung erkennt, mit der da von „einer deutschen ‚Normalisierung´" gesprochen wird, insinuierend, daß dieser nicht recht über den Weg zu trauen sei. Wir kennen die Weise, wir kennen den Text: Es ist der alte, durch die Wiedervereinigung erneuerte Vorbehalt, die Deutschen könnten wieder in zerstörerisches Unwesen verfallen, wenn ihnen nicht ihre Vergangenheit immer wieder vorgehalten werde wie das Kruzifix dem vom bösen Geiste Befallenen. Und Jürgen Habermas, unser Präzeptor Germaniae, hat sogleich Verständnishilfe geleistet, indem er in seiner Laudatio die „neue Sorte von vaterländischem Geist" beklagt hat, die sich seit 1989 im vereinigten Deutschland ausbreite. Dort verlange man nach „fraglosen Traditionen" und „starken Werten", um das Volk „zukunftsfähig" zu machen.

Ist dem so? Es ist richtig, daß eben erst die Diskussion um die Wehrmachts-Ausstellung in München solchem Verdacht Nahrung gegeben hat. Aber es darf auch nicht unterschlagen werden, daß die Reemtsma-Ausstellung das Münchener Kampffeld mit der Gloriole des Aufklärers verlassen hat, die CSU jedoch mit dem Makel des politischen Dunkelmännertums – insofern ist das Gefälle des moralischen Urteilens, notabene auch der gesinnungsstarken Scharfrichterei in der Bundesrepublik so intakt wie eh und je. Überdies macht es Mühe, die an Rabulistik grenzt, von der Vereinigung eine Spur zu solchen Zeugnissen politisch-historischer Verstocktheit zu legen. Schon gar nicht sind sie das Exempel für einen Geist, der etwa den Anspruch erhöbe, die Zukunft mitzugestalten – das geschieht auch und gerade in dem zum Bannerträger etatistischer Modernisierung gewordenen Bayern anders.

Die Wahrheit ist, daß die Vereinigung nichts so wenig hervorgebracht hat wie einen vaterländischen Geist, weder einen alten noch einen neuen, ja, daß sie überhaupt kaum etwas entzündet hat, was inspiriert und ermutigt. Das ist keine schöne Wahrheit, und selbst die Genugtuung, daß über der Vereinigung nicht einmal ein Hauch von nationalem Überschwang lag, bekommt unter diesem Gesichtspunkt einen schalen Beigeschmack. Die Unterstellung, es drohe in ihrem Sog ein Wieder-Anknüpfen an altes, verhängnisvolles Denken, hat noch weit weniger Wirklichkeit für sich wie die Vereinigung Wieder-Vereinigung ist.

Was den Argwohn gegenüber einer deutschen Normalisierung angeht, so muß man gar nicht sehr viel Sensibilität aufbringen, um für ihn Verständnis zu haben. So nahe ist uns die Dritte-Reich-Vergangenheit allemal. Gleichwohl muß es wunder nehmen, wie sehr dieses Wort eine Art untergründige Losung geworden ist, um die herum das deutsche Gegenwartsbewußtsein pendelt, wechselweise an- und abgestoßen und immer irgendwie gereizt. Kohls „Wende" von 1982/83 handelte in gewisser Weise von ihr, denn die Rückkehr zur Normalität war so etwas wie ihr Leitgedanke; im Historikerstreit markierte sie die Alarmzone der Debatte; ein gut Teil der Auseinandersetzung nach 1989 hat damit zu tun, daß sich Deutschland dem Zustand eines normalen Nationalstaats mehr angenähert hat als je zuvor in seiner Geschichte, aber sich gerade damit schwer tut. Wann werden wir gelernt haben, mit Normalität – normal umzugehen?

Hermann Rudolph, in: „Der Tagesspiegel", 16.3.1997

…und was ist mit dem „guten Deutschen"?

Als Daniel Goldhagen (37), Autor des umstrittenen Buches „Hitlers willige Vollstrecker", letzte Woche in Bonn den „Demokratiepreis 1997" erhielt, war die vorangegangene Pressekonferenz – gekommen waren unter anderen sechs Fernsehteams – gerammelt voll.

Bei der abendlichen Preisverleihung blieb in der Beethovenhalle kein Platz frei. Man sah SPD-Klose, Bonns OB Bärbel Dieckmann, die Grünen Antje Vollmer, Joschka Fischer, Kerstin Müller, den Bürgerrechtler Ullmann und PDS-Gysi.

Als eine Woche davor das Buch „Andere Deutsche unter Hitler" vorgestellt wurde – ein Buch über Deutsche, die Juden vor dem Holocaust retteten und dabei eigenes Leben riskierten –, kam ein knappes Dutzend Journalisten, keine Kamera war aufgebaut, und abgesehen vom israelischen Botschafter Primor und AA-Staatsminister Schäfer (FDP), der stellvertretend für Kinkel die Festrede hielt, fehlte die politische Prominenz – wie wohl zum Beispiel Süssmuth, Rau, Biedenkopf und Teufel Einladungen erhielten.

Der „gute" Deutsche aus der NS-Zeit steht halt nicht auf dem Spielplan des Zeitgeist-Theaters.

Corinna Hauswedell spricht für Blätter und Förderverein auf dem Empfang der Bonner Oberbürgermeisterin Barbara Dieckmann (links).
Foto: Josef Menzen

Nach einer Idee des verstorbenen jüdischen Journalisten Rolf Vogel, Bonn, aber mit neuem Konzept, schrieb der Essener Journalist Straeter über die „anderen" Deutschen (v. Hase & Koehler, 28 Mark) – bewegende Geschichten vom Bauern, der einem Juden Unterschlupf gewährte und dafür im KZ umkam, dem Chefarzt, der 17 verletzte ungarische Jüdinnen operierte und versteckte, dem Anwalt, der durch Unterlagenfälschung 2899 Juden rettete...

Fast 300 Deutsche haben sogar die Israelis im „Hain der Gerechten" bei der Gedenkstätte „Yad Vashem" namentlich geehrt, darunter Oskar Schindler.

Und bei uns? „Warum das lange Schweigen?" fragt die 88jährige Maria Althoff, die große Dame des gleichnamigen Zirkus', die mit ihrem

Mann drei Jahre eine jüdische Mutter mit zwei Töchtern und deren desertierten Vater versteckte.

Ja, warum?

Mainhardt Graf Nayhauß, in: „Bild“, 18.3.1997

„Das Verhalten der Bundesrepublik ist Anlaß zur Genugtuung“

Mitunter traute man seinen Ohren nicht. Daniel Jonah Goldhagen, dessen Buch über „Hitlers willige Vollstrecker“ wie kein anderes historisches Werk in jüngster Zeit Furore gemacht hatte und Anlaß zu heftigsten Auseinandersetzungen gewesen war, sprach jetzt in Bonn vom „Modell Deutschland“ in einem überaus positiven Sinn. Die deutsche Politik nach 1949 sei beispielhaft auch für andere Völker; sie sei weltoffen, habe aus der Geschichte gelernt und Spiegele heute einen „international verantwortungsvoll agierenden Nationalstaat“.

Den Grund für diese erstaunliche Entwicklung sah der amerikanische Historiker in der *Internationalisierung* der Bundesrepublik. Politik und Geschichtsschreibung sind für ihn nach 1945 stark „von außen“ beeinflußt worden, -sehr viel mehr jedenfalls, als dies bei anderen Staaten der Fall war. Ob von den Deutschen so gewollt oder nicht, das bleibe, so Goldhagen weiter, durchaus dahingestellt. Aber der direkte Einfluß der Siegermächte wie auch der intellektuelle Einfluß nichtdeutscher Sichtweisen haben für ihn diese Internationalisierung bewirkt, – zum Vorteil für Deutschland, zum Vorteil auch für Europa, ja eigentlich für die internationalen Beziehungen insgesamt.

Goldhagen, der sich bei seinem Deutschlandbesuch vor wenigen Monaten wegen seines umstrittenen Buches strapaziösen Kontroversen mit deutschen Historikern ausgesetzt sah, stellte jetzt in Bonn gerade der Ge-

schichtswissenschaft ein gutes Zeugnis aus: „Den Deutschen ist es am besten gelungen, eine wahrheitsgemäße Nationalgeschichte zu schreiben, weil durch die Einbeziehung nationaler wie internationaler Quellen den beschönigenden, mythologisierenden und selbsttäuschenden Tendenzen nationaler Geschichtsschreibung erfolgreich entgegengewirkt wurde."

In keinem anderen Land sei die Elite so „international orientiert" wie in der Bundesrepublik, – weder in den USA, noch in Frankreich, Italien, Großbritannien oder Japan. Das habe dann auch die Politik Bonns geprägt: „Das politische Verhalten der Bundesrepublik sollte Anlaß zur Genugtuung geben. Ihre Art, Politik zu machen, ist ein festes Merkmal der deutschen Demokratie, eine unleugbare Stärke des Landes." Und das sollte denn auch – zum Nutzen Deutscher und Nichtdeutscher – beibehalten werden: „Die Grundlagen der Bonner Republik und ihres Erfolgs, darunter ihr außergewöhnliches Selbstverständnis und ihre außergewöhnliche politische Praxis, müssen auf die Berliner Republik übertragen werden."

Das alles relativiere nicht sein Buch über Hitler und die Deutschen. Der Nationalsozialismus, so sagte es Goldhagen sehr dezidiert, war kein Betriebsunfall der deutschen Geschichte. Und er bleibe *das* zentrale Ereignis der modernen deutschen Geschichte.

Goldhagen hatte in Bonn den Demokratiepreis 1997 der „Blätter für deutsche und internationale Politik" erhalten. Zur Laudatio waren der Hamburger Sozialwissenschaftler Jan Philipp Reemtsma und der Frankfurter Philosoph und Sozialforscher Jürgen Habermas in die Bundesstadt gekommen. Beide gingen dann doch vorrangig auf Goldhagens Buch ein und setzten sich mit den vielfältigen Reaktionen darauf in Wissenschaft und Öffentlichkeit auseinander. Habermas sah manche Reaktion besonders kritisch: „Diese kritische Einstellung gegenüber Eigenem ist es, was Goldhagens Studie fördert – und was die Besorgnis mancher Konservativer auf den Plan ruft ... Seit 1989 festigt sich im vereinigten Deutschland eine neue Sorte von vaterländischem Geist, dem die Lernprozesse der letzten Jahrzehnte schon „zu weit" gehen.

Reaktionen, Stellungnahmen und Argumente Spiegelten doch, so Habermas, immer auch den inneren Zustand der Demokratie: „Wie wir Schuld und Unschuld im historischen Rückblick verteilt sehen, Spiegelt

auch die Normen, nach denen wir uns gegenseitig als Bürger dieser Republik zu achten willens sind." Und das sei denn auch Goldhagens eigentliches Verdienst: Nicht auf Universalien oder auf Unveränderliches habe er die Aufmerksamkeit gerichtet, sondern letztlich auf Faktoren, „die durch einen Bewußtseinswandel verändert werden können."

Demokratie und offener Diskurs also als Chance. Der Abend in der Beethovenhalle stimmte jedenfalls hoffnungsvoll. Man hatte die Stuhlreihen eng zusammengerückt, um wenigstens 2000 Zuhörern Platz zu bieten; zweimal soviel Interessenten mußte man zuvor absagen. Der Abend dauerte dann – mit den drei konzentrierten Reden, zwei Musikstücken und ohne Pause – von 20 bis 22.30 Uhr; keine Unruhe kam auf, keine Müdigkeit; das überwiegend jüngere Publikum zeigte sich dem Anspruch durchaus gewachsen.

Dirk Klose, in: „Das Parlament",21.3.1997

Geschichtswunder

„Was in der Bundesrepublik erreicht wurde, ist von großem Gewicht und, im Hinblick auf die kulturelle und politische Praxis, durchaus als Leitbild zu empfehlen." Diese Worte von Daniel Goldhagen anläßlich der Verleihung des Demokratie-Preises der *Blätter für deutsche und internationale Politik* bestätigen „den Deutschen" einen vorbildlichen Umgang mit ihrer Geschichte. Sie haben aus der Vergangenheit gelernt und avancieren zum internationalen Vorbild – dem Holocaust sei Dank. Nach dem Wirtschaftswunder nun also ein Geschichtswunder? Aus psychoanalytischer Sicht liegt der Verdacht nahe, daß dem begrüßenswerten Perspektivenwechsel in der Historiographie des Nationalsozialismus im Verlauf der „Goldhagen-Debatte' latent ein Moment von Gegenaufklärung innewohnt, das destruktive Wirkungen auf diesen Diskurs entfalten könnte.

Zunächst ist davon auszugehen, daß die Auseinandersetzung mit dem Nationalsozialismus notwendig von unbewußten Abwehrmechanismen

begleitet ist. Die Massenvernichtung stellt nach Dan Diner einen universellen Zivilisationsbruch dar, eine fundamentale Infragestellung von Rationalität und Moral. Die Abwehr ist daher nicht (nur) als moralisch zu bewertende Unwilligkeit anzusehen, sondern vielmehr als unbewußter psychischer Schutzversuch vor der tiefgreifenden Erschütterung der Grundlagen alltäglichen Handelns und Denkens. Saul Friedländer beschreibt eine der Historiographie des Nationalsozialismus innewohnende „temptation of closure"; der Versuchung, die Geschichte abzuschließen, unterliegt jede Erinnerung an dieses Ereignis. Diese dialektische Bewegung des Erinnerungsprozesses, der ein Vergessen erst ermöglicht und befördert, erscheint besonders prekär angesichts eines historischen Ereignisses, das gerade nicht dem Vergessen anheimfallen soll.

Die unausweichliche Dialektik von Erinnern und Vergessen nötigt zu einer kritischen Anfrage an die Funktion von Erinnerung und Geschichtskonstruktion, in diesem Fall an die Funktion der Goldhagen-Debatte. Hier scheint der *latente* Wunsch, die Geschichte abzuschließen, eine wesentliche Rolle zu spielen, und zwar nicht unter den dezidierten Gegnern von Goldhagens Thesen, sondern vielmehr beim überwiegend zustimmenden, jüngeren Teil des Publikums. Wie konnte Goldhagen mit seinem radikalen Erklärungsmuster eines spezifisch deutschen eliminatorischen Antisemitismus zum Sympathieträger der Nachkriegsgenerationen werden? Die Universalität des Zivilisationsbruchs wird dabei unbewußt verleugnet. Die Geschichte wird zwar anerkannt, verliert aber ihre Bedeutung als fundamentale Infragestellung im Sinne Dan Diners.

Dies liegt an der Form, in der die Debatte sich vollzog und die man als religiöse Inszenierung beschreiben könnte. Eine psychische Funktion von Religion besteht nach Freud in der Sinnstiftung; sie verspricht Antworten auf die Rätsel menschlicher Existenz wie Tod, Ursprung und Sinn des Lebens. Mit seiner ebenso schlichten wie plausiblen Argumentation offeriert Goldhagen eine Erklärung für das Unbegreifliche der Massenvernichtung und beendet damit die drängende Frage, wie sie möglich gewesen sein konnte. Insofern liefert er einen empirischen Beleg für die von Friedländer problematisierte Tendenz, er nivelliert in positivistischer Weise den erkenntnistheoretischen Bruch und benennt das Undetermi-

nierte. Eine weitere Funktion von Religion liegt in der Vorstellung von Erlösung, die einen Ausweg aus dem unausweichlichen Schuldzusammenhang eröffnet. Diese Funktion wird virulent durch die Aktualisierung unbewußter Schuld- und Schamgefühle, die aufgrund der transgenerationalen Weitergabe latenter Identifizierungen auch bei den Nachkriegsgenerationen bestehen. Verstärkt werden diese Schuldgefühle durch das Erklärungsmuster eines spezifisch deutschen Antisemitismus aufgrund der (unbewußten) Identifizierung mit dieser Kultur.

Diesem psychischen Konflikt begegnet Goldhagen mit seiner wiederholten Bestätigung, daß „die Deutschen“ heute anders seien als ihre Vorfahren. Das macht ihn zum Stellvertreter der Anklagen der jüngeren Generationen an die älteren, was der Abgrenzung und Distanzierung ebenso dient wie der Bestätigung moralischer Uberlegenheit. Die Geschichtskonstruktion wird so zu einem Instrument des Generationenkonflikts. Dabei bleibt jedoch die zentrale Frage offen, worin der Wandel dieser doch so tief verwurzelten Mentalität gründet. Folgt man Goldhagens Argumentation, kann dieser Wandel nur durch Auschwitz verursacht sein. Danach wäre Auschwitz der absolute, unvorstellbare Exzeß des deutschen Antisemitismus, der zugleich diese fatale Tradition bricht. Der „Holocaust“ würde zu einem Opfer – entsprechend der ursprünglichen griechischen Bedeutung, das die Deutschen von ihrem spezifischen, eliminatorischen Antisemitismus befreit. Das klingt zynisch angesichts der Millionen Ermordeten und des anhaltenden Leidens der Überlebenden; die immense Publizität von Goldhagens Thesen könnte aber auf dieses entlastende Moment zurückzuführen sein. Der Autor erscheint als Erlöser, der „die Deutschen“ aus ihrem historischen Schuldzusammenhang befreit.

Häufig wird in Deutschland im Kontext der Auseinandersetzung mit dem Nationalsozialismus der Beginn eines chassidischen Sprichworts zitiert:“Das Geheimnis der Erlösung heißt Erinnerung.“ Diese religiöse Dimension von Erinnerung birgt die Hoffnung, die Geschichte abschließen zu können und damit die Gefahr ihrer Instrumentalisierung für die eigenen unbewußten Wünsche.

Ilka Quindeau, in: „Frankfurter Rundschau“, 1.4.1997